MARKETING
EDUCATION

MARKETING
EDUCATION

Lynton Gray

OPEN UNIVERSITY PRESS
Milton Keynes · Philadelphia

Open University Press
Celtic Court
22 Ballmoor
Buckingham
MK18 1XW

and
1900 Frost Road, Suite 101
Bristol, PA 19007, USA

First published 1991

British Library Cataloguing-in-Publication Data

Gray, Lynton
    Marketing education.
    I. Title
    370.19068

    ISBN 0–335–09676–X
    ISBN 0–335–09675–1 pbk

Library of Congress Cataloging-in-Publication Data

Gray, Lynton.
        Marketing education/Lynton Gray.
            p.   cm.
        Includes bibliographical references and index.
        ISBN 0–335–09676–X   ISBN 0–335–09675–1 pbk
            1. Education–Marketing.   2. Public relations–Schools.   3. Public
    relations–Universities and colleges.   I. Title.
    LB2806.G675 1991
    370'.68'8–dc20   91–14701
                                                                                             CIP

Typeset by Inforum Typesetting, Portsmouth
Printed and bound in Great Britain by
Woolnough Bookbinding, Irthlingborough

Contents

Acknowledgements

I am grateful to all my colleagues and students at the Polytechnic of East London and The Staff College with whom I have shared ideas about marketing, developed and delivered marketing courses, and prepared marketing strategies over the past few years. I have also learned a great deal from friends and colleagues in The Marketing Network, and would like to thank them for their enthusiasm and commitment.

I would like to thank Kevin Gavaghan, Marketing Director of Midland Bank for his help and insightful ideas, and Middlesex Polytechnic for permission to reproduce the advertisement in Figure 12. Keith Scribbins and Peter Davies at The Staff College were among the first to recognize the importance of marketing in education, and I owe much to their pioneer work and to their continuing efforts to improve the quality of educational marketing. Finally, I must express my gratitude to Mary Gray for her practical insights, continuing examples of effective educational marketing and constant support.

1 | Why educational organizations are concerned about marketing

Introduction

This book is written for all those with an interest in improving the quality of our education service. As the book makes clear, this includes not only education managers – principals, head teachers, departmental heads and the like – but also parents, governors and all those teaching and non-teaching staff who are facing up to turbulent and often uncomfortable changes in their daily work. It is written particularly for the sake of the education service's prime customers – its pupils and students. The vision of marketing which permeates the following pages is one which is concerned centrally with improving their experiences of formal education.

This is not an 'academic' text that attempts merely to describe or explain the current interest in and concern for educational marketing. Nor is it a collection of tips and recipes to be tried out uncritically by harassed managers. It is rather an attempt to provide a set of perspectives to help all those wanting to use marketing ideas. These might be related to readers' own experiences and then adapted to their needs.

It also tries to reassure all those worried that marketing might damage education by introducing alien notions and harmful practices. To this end, it looks right across the spectrum of education sectors – from higher education to nursery schools – at ways in which marketing is currently being employed and might be more effectively used as a vehicle for improvement. By exploring most corners of the educational jungle, and by looking outside education to other public and private sectors, it is intended to provoke argument and stimulate ideas. Its major purpose is to improve educational provision and practice, in the belief that where marketing becomes integrated as a central aspect of school and college management, the other elements of management are improved. In turn, this will improve the range and quality of the institution's educational provision.

It is important to emphasize from the outset that marketing is a great deal more than the advertising and the other 'selling' activities that many people still associate with the term. The definition which comes closest to the spirit of this book is that of the Institute of Marketing: 'A management process responsible for anticipating, identifying and then satisfying consumer wants and needs with a view to making profit.'

The notion of profit is not one that fits in comfortably with a public sector service, and its equivalents in such a service are considered in the next chapter. The essence of this definition is the central idea of making management decisions, including the investment of resources, in order to seek identifiable benefits for those making use of the service – the pupils and students.

The book starts from two assumptions. The first is that any organization benefits from the careful examination of the needs of its clients and customers. The second is that services such as the education service are particularly vulnerable when they fail to listen to their customers. It argues and demonstrates that educational organizations need to reflect upon their relationships with customers and those who sponsor customers, starting from the recognition that those who use their services *are* customers with needs, rights and expectations. The book scrutinizes the ways in which institutions listen to and inform their customers (students) and those who act directly on their behalf to determine forms of educational provision – normally parents and employers. It indicates ways in which schools, colleges and other educational organizations can examine whether they are sufficiently responsive to the needs of customers and their sponsors, and means by which they might improve the quality of the services they provide by developing more structured and carefully planned strategies for marketing those services.

Before going further, some short mention of terminology is needed. Words such as 'client', 'customer' and 'consumer' are used fairly loosely in service industries. It is possible to distinguish between a 'client' as someone who buys the personal services of a professional person such as a lawyer in what is a relatively long-term relationship, and a 'customer' whose transactions are short-term or with a non-professional service such as a shop. A further distinction can be made between both client and customer on the one hand as those who buy goods and services and the 'consumer' who consumes the goods or uses the service without necessarily selecting or paying for it. Thus children are 'consumers' of the food bought for them by their parents as 'customers' of shops.

Such distinctions are not clear-cut in the education service. Oxbridge students receiving individual tuition from their tutor might be perceived as 'clients', but the same hardly applies to students attending a conference at which the same tutor is lecturing. Parents may act as 'customers' in deciding on the primary school to be attended by their children, the 'consumers'. But the same is not so true at the age of 11 or 12 when the students usually have some say in the decision as to which secondary school to attend, and is even less true at the ages of 16 or 18 when decisions regarding further and higher education are made. To avoid confusion, therefore, the term 'customer' is used throughout the book to describe students and those acting on their behalf – normally parents and those employers who select vocational education and training courses for their workers. The word 'consumer' is used occasionally where it seems more appropriate, but from now on the word 'client' will be avoided.

Schools and colleges have always marketed themselves. Until recently, this has been done patchily, apologetically and instinctively. There has been little formal organization, minimal expenditure and only occasional reference to those canons of marketing which shape the marketing operations of industrial and commercial organizations. This is now changing rapidly. Further and higher education has been exhorted to market itself more professionally, and parts have responded with energy and enthusiasm to the challenge. The schools sectors now face similar challenges, which are looked at later in this chapter. Schools and colleges now look to marketing in order to increase their resources, or at least to compensate for resource reductions. The following chapters suggest ways in which this might be achieved. They also provide warnings that, unless questions of quality of service are addressed, those extra resources are unlikely to be forthcoming.

No attempt is made here to propose the imposition of alien approaches from the worlds of industry and advertising on to educational organizations. Those resistant to the view that the education service will improve as soon as it follows the more 'business-like' approaches of the private sectors can be reassured: such naïve and simplistic views are not peddled here. While there is much that the education service can learn from the private sector (and from other parts of the public sector), there are no easy recipes for improvement, and no ideas which can be lifted wholesale and transported into schools and colleges. However, the next chapters do suggest ways in which the education service might make use of principles and concepts underpinning the marketing of some commercial services, as well as drawing attention to limitations of such adaptations from the private sectors.

Examples of private sector service industries with some features not too dissimilar from aspects of public sector education are discussed in the next chapter. There seems no good reason to re-invent marketing wheels when solutions to similar problems to those now faced by education are available for scrutiny and adaptation. Similarly, I hope that some of the home-grown approaches to marketing, developed by schools and colleges and discussed in later chapters, are sufficiently novel and distinctive to be of interest to non-educational organizations. The passage of ideas – even about marketing – between public and private sectors in Britain is not a one-way street.

Later chapters explore some of the initiatives, ideas and theories currently influencing the marketing of educational services. Chapter 3 spells out some basic principles underpinning any form of marketing and applies these with examples to the marketing endeavours of schools and colleges. Chapters 4 and 5 indicate ways in which educational organizations might go about two fundamental tasks: the development of marketing policies and marketing plans (Chapter 4) and the collection and use of information (Chapter 5). The next three chapters look in some detail at key components of a successful marketing strategy: the achievement of an appropriate 'marketing mix'. Chapter 6 looks at courses and other services, the places where they are delivered and the prices charged. Chapter 7 examines promotion and public relations, while Chapter 8 considers the people delivering the services. Chapter 9 looks at ways of creating and maintaining an organizational framework and climate in which marketing is properly supported and encouraged, and at strategies for generating income. The book concludes with some suggestions as to ways in which the education service might develop new approaches to the marketing of educational services which derive from sound educational practice.

The book is written after most of the changes introduced into England and Wales by the 1988 Education Reform Act have begun to take effect. It is obviously heavily influenced by the Act and its clones in Scotland and Northern Ireland. These Acts have established new ground rules for education in which effective marketing has become an important requirement for every educational organization. The book recognizes that most of these changes are paralleled by similar changes in education systems throughout the world. Concerns for value for money, greater accountability and deregulation are in no way uniquely British. Nor is the belief that the consumers of public education and those who speak for them should have more say in the nature and quality of that provision: we still lag behind a number of Western countries in this respect. Experiences of working with educational institutions and systems in many parts of the world throughout the 1980s are drawn upon in an attempt not only to reflect upon overseas parallels to some British approaches to marketing education, but also to suggest ways in which we might learn from the experience of others.

New initiatives, new problems

Two clearly expressed objectives have dominated central government policy for the British education services over the past decade. The first has been to wrest control of the service from the 'providers' (teachers and their professional associations and the local education authorities) and shift control to consumers (parents, employers and communities) and to central government agencies, particularly the Departments of Education and Employment. The second objective has been to improve efficiency by increasing competition in the public sector, an explicit purpose of the 1988 Education Reform Act. One important benefit sought in this way has been some reduction in public expenditure by reducing waste and promoting the notion of 'value for money'.

The consequence of these policies has been to inject a number of features of a 'market economy' into public sector education. Two new categories of schools have been established to compete with local authority-provided schools: city technology colleges and grant-maintained schools, both funded directly from the Department of Education and Science (DES). In the post-school sectors, the allocation of funds by the Department of Employment (until recently through its Training Agency) has encouraged the proliferation of private training organizations in competition with further education colleges. Such competition has recently been intensified by the privatization of part of the Training Agency itself, with the management buy-out of its 'Skills Training Agency', and by the establishment of 80–100 Training and Enterprise Councils, funded by the government but run along business lines by business people, and taking over the bulk of the Training Agency's responsibilities for vocational training. Market conditions in higher education have been simulated by the two government-controlled central funding organizations, which have initiated forms of competitive bidding for limited resources.

Underlying and intensifying all this government-promoted competition has been the impact of major demographic change. The total population of young people in Britain has declined by up to one-third since the 1970s. First primary schools, then secondary schools and now the post-school sectors have either had to compete for a reduced number of potential customers or face contraction or even closure. Since the wholesale destruction of the teacher education sector in the late 1970s, schools and colleges have generally managed to avoid closure, with the result that institutions are now generally smaller and more competitive than they were a decade ago. The 1988 legislation has made it even easier to resist planned closure, by offering schools the opportunity to 'opt out' of local authority control. Many have taken this option in order to avoid proposed closure. Market forces have, in consequence, replaced local government planning as the prime means by which the numbers of schools might be reduced in response to reductions in the size of the age groups they serve.

Schools and colleges are, not surprisingly in this climate, becoming more responsive to their customers. A later section of this chapter outlines some manifestations of this. Government policies have attempted to promote greater responsiveness and greater accountability to consumers by initiating (in the 1986 Education Act) annual parents' meetings at which governing bodies must report on and justify school policies and plans. Parents also have the opportunity, when such meetings are quorate, to pass resolutions which must be heeded by governing bodies. Membership of these bodies has been manipulated in order to increase further such responsiveness. The proportion of parents, business and community representatives has been increased at the expense of local authority representation and (in the post-school sectors) staff and student representation. This movement for a stronger consumer voice in education has been supported by organizations and publications which articulate consumerist views. The Advisory Centre for Education, a pressure group to increase the education service's responsiveness to its customers, and its monthly *ACE Bulletin*, have long advised parents and parent-governors as to their rights and responsibilities. Similar support and pressure has come from the National Association for Governors and Managers (NAGM) and from local organizations articulating the views of parents and governors. In higher education, the National Union of Students (NUS) has long argued stridently for the rights of the sector's customers, although attempts to establish similar voices to articulate the views of younger students have been unsuccessful.

Recent reforms of the UK's much criticized training system have given even more prominence to the voice of employers as consumers. The establishment of some 100 new Training and Enterprise Councils (TECs) and, in Scotland, Local Enterprise Councils (LECs), transferred the major part of central government's training expenditure, until now disbursed by the Training Agency, to non-elected boards comprising for the most part business community representatives. Their task is to control a £3 billion training budget spent according to TEC/LEC determination in further education colleges, private training organizations and the in-house training units of employers themselves. It is probably the clearest demonstration to date in the UK of a government philosophy which believes that the business world not only is best-placed as a prime consumer of education and training to state what it wants, but also has the collective skills to be able to obtain what it asks for.

The closer involvement of both parents and employers in education decisions has been accompanied by tight constraints on available public funds for schools and colleges. This has encouraged institutions to develop ways of persuading parents and employers to make good the shortfall of resources. Schools have become adept at persuading parents to support fund-raising events, and some of the more effective techniques here are discussed in Chapter 9. Schools and colleges have sought sponsorship from employers, while colleges, universities and polytechnics have generated income from the sale of training, consultancy, research and other services to private sector and governmental organizations. Meanwhile, institutions have explored ways in which they might generate income from other, non-educational activities such as hiring out their premises.

The government's attempts to transform education from a provider-dominated service to one in which the consumer's voice is paramount culminated in the 1988 Education Reform Act (for England and Wales) and the similar legislation in Northern Ireland (the Education Reform Order) and in Scotland (the Self Governing Schools, etc. Act, known as the 'Etcetera Act'). The deregulation elements of this legislation have their parallels in a number of countries, as part of a worldwide trend towards shifting responsibilities to individual educational institutions. Caldwell and Spinks (1988) describe some of these, including developments in Australia and North America. In the UK, as elsewhere, these involve the delegation of both financial and employer responsibilities to schools and colleges – or more precisely to their governing bodies or equivalent.

The processes of 'local management of schools/colleges' have greatly stimulated interest in marketing approaches. The legislation has introduced a form of voucher system, whereby the resources obtained by schools and colleges are directly related to the institutions' ability to attract students. Each school pupil brings with him or her an annual sum, fixed according to a local education authority (LEA) formula approved by central government. The situation in colleges, polytechnics and universities is rather more complicated because of the variety of modes of attendance and the different costs of different types of course (with engineering and agriculture courses requiring more resources than humanities or business studies). It is complicated still further by governmental attempts to retain some central planning controls by means of target numbers and recruitment ceilings. These are residual features of a centrally planned system, but they operate in an artificially created market environment, so that universities and polytechnics are now required to tender competitively for money to run specific courses for stated numbers of students.

The basic principle throughout most of the British education systems, as in many other parts of the world, is that institutions will increase their total resources if they recruit more students. Conversely, failure to recruit expected numbers of students will result in a loss of anticipated resources.

This is a crude input-based market system that focuses attention on the recruitment of students. Other countries have developed more sophisticated output-based approaches, which switch attention to the successful completion of programmes by students. Recent reforms in the Dutch educational system provide examples of this approach. In marketing terms, recruitment becomes less important than retention and customer satisfaction in an output-based system. There are some signs that parts of the English system are showing interest in output-based resourcing. The new TECs in England and Wales, and the LECs in Scotland, are now managing a new government-funded voucher system of 'training credits' for 16- to 19-year-olds, and there is at least a possibility that the vouchers will be related not to input but to successful completion of training programmes. If this principle is extended further it will have a very substantial influence upon the nature and direction of educational marketing, focusing less on recruitment and more on retention and customer satisfaction.

School and college responses to marketing pressures

The scale and complex nature of the education system makes it difficult to generalize about how individual institutions, or even the different sectors, have responded to the pressures and changes outlined above. A number of trends and developments can be spotted, and these are referred to below. Many of their characteristic features are considered in greater detail in the following chapters.

There is little doubt that increased competition has led to more consideration throughout the country's schools and colleges of the wishes and interests of customers and their parents and employers. Back in 1980, government legislation required schools to prepare brochures for parents giving details of the educational services on offer. Many schools had already produced such brochures. Others looked at them with suspicion, believing that they were introducing alien commercial advertising approaches which would waste resources and divert attention from basic educational tasks. Many LEAs shared this latter view and responded to the legislation by placing constraints on schools wanting to use their brochures as vehicles for promoting their schools, by requiring a standardized approach by all schools. The 1988 legislation has freed schools in England and Wales from such LEA restrictions. Meanwhile, with few such inhibitions, further education colleges, polytechnics and universities have produced increasingly professional prospectuses, whose characteristics are examined in Chapter 7. These institutions, of course, lie outside the compulsory education system, so depend upon voluntary decisions by students who not only could choose another college, but could decide to enter the world of work or a government training scheme instead of going to college.

Some of the strongest manifestations of a more responsive approach by schools and colleges have come, however, from the compulsory sectors. They include the gradual disappearance of an attitude to parents embodied in those notorious notices to primary school parents requiring that 'parents must not cross the white line' at the far side of the playground, when waiting for their children to come out of school. Many primary schools have worked hard and enthusiastically to develop a genuine sense of partnership with parents. 'Toddlers' Clubs' for infants below school age have encouraged parents to come into the school, and to keep their youngsters at that school when they reach school age. Parents are invited into classrooms both as visitors and to work alongside and in support of children, and many primary schools have used an empty classroom (once rolls have fallen sufficiently to give some free space) as a 'parents' room', where they can meet with friends and wait in comfort for their children.

Other aspects of change in the primary sector – which was the first sector other than teacher training to cope with falling rolls – can be seen on entering primary schools. They are commonly brighter, more welcoming and more clearly signposted than institutions catering for older students. The creative display of pupil and teacher work is used to enhance the quality of the environment – a lesson only just now being learned by some secondary schools and further education colleges and still apparently not recognized in some institutions of higher education. Many primary schools have been able to augment their meagre finances by fundraising events which have enabled them to double their expenditure on books and consumable materials.

In the post-school sectors, finance from the Department of Employment (formerly via the Manpower Services Commission, then the Training Agency) has stimulated colleges' marketing responses. Many colleges have received funding to appoint (commonly for an initial year) staff with responsibility for marketing, as is discussed in Chapter 9. Employment Department funding also led to a major action research project, based at the Further Education Staff College, designed to improve the quality of marketing throughout the further education sector. This 'Responsive College Programme' led to the publication of a multi-media training pack (Theodossin, 1989) whose uses are considered in later chapters.

In higher education, experience of cut-throat marketing and ferocious competition has been gained overseas. The abrupt increase in overseas students' fees a decade ago sharply reduced the numbers of overseas students attending UK colleges. It opened up markets traditionally served by UK higher education to other countries, including the USA, Canada, Australia and several European nations. UK institutions have had to work hard to win back some of the business lost by what is now generally recognized as a short-sighted and mistaken government decision. They have come up against the professional marketing strategies of rival North American institutions, and have had to develop new skills and techniques in order to compete. Some of these techniques have been criticized for introducing some of the less savoury attributes of the commercial marketing world into educational marketing.

Other manifestations of the capacity of the education service to respond to the political and social changes of the past decade are examined in subsequent chapters. In general, educational institutions have been given new responsibilities and have shown a good deal of initiative, despite limited resources, in responding to some of the challenges contained in the new systems imposed upon them. Attitudes which consider marketing to be an unacceptable intrusion of the business world into the purer environment of education are diminishing but can still readily be uncovered. However, the recognition that schools and colleges need to employ marketing strategies if they are to survive and flourish is now found in all education sectors and in most institutions. In other words, the awareness of marketing as a force for good is there. What is not yet well developed is a clear view of the most effective ways in which educational marketing might be undertaken. Nor is there as yet a clear perspective on the place of marketing within an educational organization: it is still regarded as a temporary intruder or a bolted-on extra. The following chapters spell out a number of ways forward, from a perspective which emphasizes that marketing should be fully integrated with other aspects of institutional management, in order to improve the quality of service provided by the school or college.

2 | Marketing service industries

This chapter starts from the premise that education is a service and so has a number of features in common with other activities in the public and private sectors which provide services. It examines the differences between the marketing of services and the marketing of products, as in manufacturing industry, and then looks at the distinctive approaches to the marketing of services which characterize service industries. It goes on to examine two specific service industries in the private sector (tourism and banking), which have features and problems resembling some of those in the education service. In examining aspects of the marketing of these services, it raises questions about the applicability of such private sector approaches when applied to educational marketing, before making some suggestions for ways in which educational institutions might look at and adapt ideas taken from other service industries.

The basic principles of marketing derive from the marketing of industrial products such as cars and consumer durables. The standard textbooks (e.g. Kotler, 1986; Cameron *et al.*, 1988) emphasize these industrial and commercial examples, and posit a rational marketing sequence of activities, as summarized in Fig. 1.

Thus an organization identifies the need to market a new product, or improve the marketing of a product whose sales are declining or otherwise causing problems. It therefore undertakes a marketing audit, identifying distinctive market segments and their

Marketing needs/problems
↓
Marketing research and audit
↓
Marketing planning
↓
The marketing mix
↓
Marketing strategies and tactics

Fig. 1   A basic marketing management model.

characteristics, and carries out forms of marketing research into the preferences and expectations of a sample of those market segments, exploring marketing opportunities in existing and new markets. On the basis of the evidence from the audit and the marketing research, a marketing plan is drawn up, which spells out selected target markets and predicted demand rates. Central to the plan is the notion of the 'marketing mix' of the '4 Ps' – *product*, *place*, *price* and *promotion*. Each of these provides the basis for a marketing strategy, in order to achieve an effective balance of marketing activities. The organization then implements the marketing plan by means of an agreed set of major strategies and detailed tactics. Davies and Scribbins (1985) demonstrate clearly the application of this approach to the marketing of further and higher education. Its value lies largely in the systematic nature of the approach, the emphasis given to the collection of evidence through research and audit, and the clear demonstration that marketing amounts to a lot more than selling, advertising and public relations.

Characteristics of service industries

While this marketing model might be wholly appropriate for many manufacturing industries, its applicability both within the public sector and in service industries has been questioned (Cowell, 1984). For a start the model is structured around the concept of a 'product' – something tangible, with an identifiable manufacturing cost and a clearly marketable image. The success of the marketing function can, therefore, be measured in relation to the profitability of the manufacturing company and, more precisely, in terms of the numbers of items sold and the gap between the manufacturing cost and the sale price. A service industry does not sell a tangible product as such at all. A standard definition of a 'service' emphasizes its intangibility.

> A service is any activity or benefit that one party can offer to another that is essentially intangible and does not result in the ownership of anything. . . . They cannot be seen, tasted, felt, heard or smelled before they are bought. (Kotler, 1986)

The distinction between products and services is not clear-cut. Some services provide a product as part of the service (e.g. a car hire firm). Others combine tangible products in complex ways with an intangible ambience (e.g. a restaurant meal). The distinction between products and services is perhaps better seen as a tangible–intangible spectrum. From such a perspective, education is right at the 'intangible' end of the spectrum, with few if any tangible products normally provided as part of the service. Many services take steps to provide tangible benefits along with the service in order to encourage customers to perceive more clearly the benefits they have received – and to remind them of the benefits after the service has been provided.

Kotler (1986) goes on to add three other basic characteristics of services to that of *intangibility*. He draws attention to their *variability*, depending upon who provides them and the time and place of delivery, to their *perishability* (an empty cinema seat is income lost forever) and to their *inseparability* from their providers.

The nature and quality of any service are *inseparable* from the service's providers. Services cannot exist in isolation from the people (or machines) who provide them. This constrains industries where the service provider is a scarce resource, e.g. a highly skilled surgeon, lawyer, entertainer or engineer. Attempts to overcome such limitations include replacing people by machines – much easier now that computers can provide so many services from vehicle and health diagnosis to cash disbursement. Other approaches include increasing the numbers of people able to receive the service at any one time (larger classes and boxing matches on satellite television) and reducing the time spent in delivering the service (high-speed trains and one-stop shopping).

Other services approach this differently by featuring the provider as a distinctive benefit of the service, as in the restaurant owned by a famous chef, the holiday package led by a member of the aristocracy, and most notably in the entertainment industry, where the sight and sound of the provider *is* the unique benefit.

Variability derives in part from the concept of inseparability. The service depends upon the quality of the providers, whether human or machine. Service organizations commonly try to reduce this variability by introducing forms of quality control and standardized procedures, with the consequence that identical responses can be found from personnel throughout the country working for a particular car hire firm, chain-store or bank – whose premises also look exactly the same.

The concept of *perishability* means that an excess of demand over supply cannot be met by playing a football cup final on successive days to satisfy all who want to watch it. Education shares with airlines, theatres, hotels and sports stadia the problems of occupancy, whether of seats, rooms or classroom desks. Education, despite the Audit Commission's (1984) quantification of surplus seats in secondary schools at £230 per place per year, not only has yet to develop appropriate strategies, but is ambivalent as to whether perishability is indeed a problem at all. Empty seats in a classroom might now mean lost income for the institution, but this is such a new phenomenon that its impact has not yet pervaded the education service. Empty seats mean smaller classes and less pressures on the teachers. The notion that the smaller the class the better the educational quality is persistent and supported with some research evidence. The private sector of education takes advantage of this by making a promotional feature of small classes – and charging accordingly. But for most pupils and students education in a small class is an unexpected and probably unsought quasi-benefit.

The application of marketing approaches in service industries is a relatively recent phenomenon. Until recently, service organizations in the UK and the USA were being criticized for being insufficiently market-oriented. Marketing has been restricted or banned by the professional codes of some service sectors. The rapid growth of other sectors has meant that they have not felt the need to market their services, with demand well in excess of supply. These barriers are now disappearing, but, as they do so, service organizations are learning that the classic market approaches of the producers of goods do not necessarily offer obvious strategies for the marketing of services. In particular, the inability of service industries to promote a standard, tangible, storable product has rendered inapplicable some of the standard marketing prescriptions. However, some service industries have substantial experience of successful marketing: the lessons of two of these are considered next.

Banking and tourism are well-established industries whose services are intangible, perishable, variable and inseparable from the service providers. They are examined here to investigate whether they have some lessons for the education service, without necessarily prescribing the details of an appropriate marketing strategy. Their location in the private sector means that there are substantial differences from public (or 'non-profit') organizations, and these differences are considered when drawing analogies between these industries and the education service.

The tourism and travel industry

The tourism and travel industry shares with education the problem that its customers believe that they know more about the industry than those who work for it. It also resembles education in that it offers intangible, unmeasurable outcomes in terms of future well-being that cannot be guaranteed. While both services can describe in general terms the processes to be undertaken in order to achieve those outcomes, neither can offer many guarantees about those processes, whether they be uncrowded beaches, congenial company or exciting classes. The confident expectations aroused by the purchase of a new Volvo do not necessarily apply when signing up for a holiday or a training course.

There is, therefore, an element of risk in deciding which of a wide range of possible options to select. People sign up for a holiday, as they do for a course of study, without knowing except in the most general sense what they are going to receive. The activities to be undertaken might be anticipated, but the outcomes are far less clear. The likely benefits of a number of GCSE grades or a second-class honours degree are at least as difficult to quantify as the consequences of a fortnight in Lanzarote. The achievement of the expected outcome cannot be guaranteed when offering the service, whether it be a sun-tan or a BTEC Higher National Diploma. The tourist industry takes steps to minimize the sense of risk, while maintaining a sense of novelty, partly by the device of the package tour, whereby participants stay together with 'their own kind' and have only limited contact with unfamiliar foods, languages and cultures. The travel firm's guide or courier is the local manifestation of the service, available to resolve difficulties, offer assurances and draw attention to benefits. Schools and colleges use 'form' or 'year' tutors and counsellors in very similar roles.

The tourism and travel industry is as much concerned with regulating consumer demand as it is with generating that demand. Much of the marketing effort is devoted to trying to shift demand from the peak season to the off-peak and intermediate 'shoulder' seasons. Education attempts to regulate demand by establishing entry criteria, normally in the form of entry qualifications. Devices used in the travel industry to regulate demand by price, for example with discounts for off-peak travel, have as yet few education equivalents.

In order to match demand and supply, travel and tourism invest heavily in marketing research. The industry needs information about its customers and the ways in which its market can be 'segmented' in terms of age, economic status, social class and geographical distribution. Market research is used, first to identify the characteristic features of these groups which make them distinctive 'market segments', and then to ascertain their changing tastes and preferences. The information thus collected is used both to tailor provision to the tastes of specified segments, and to market available services in terms most likely to appeal to selected segments, particularly when this involves trying to shift demand away from the peak season or from popular locations where demand exceeds supply.

Evidence from market research, then, enables the industry to 'brand' particular kinds of service or package to appeal to identified market segments. Thus major tour operators such as Thomson Holidays use a range of brand names whose brochures demonstrate their distinctive target markets. The brand names then feature prominently in the publicity materials, in an attempt to associate particular kinds of benefit with particular brand names. The lessons for education from these approaches point first to the efforts needed to reduce both risk and confusion when there are many alternatives available, and then to the need to emphasize likely benefits. Contrast the problems faced by a 16-year-old having to choose between BTEC, CGLI, CPVE, TVEI, 'A' levels or NVQs at the local sixth form college, further education college or school sixth form. The decisions are probably a lot more important than whether to holiday on Mykonos or Ibiza, but the enticements of the holiday options are likely to be more clearly presented than the educational choices. For a start, the tour operators' publicity materials are likely to be designed professionally, written with benefits in mind, and distributed to reach those most likely to make the key holiday decisions.

Both tourism and education face the service industry problem of perishability or lost sales. The unsold car can be stored in a showroom and its price manipulated until a purchaser is found. The unsold seat, whether in an aircraft or a classroom, is lost forever, so that service industries have the double-edged problem of an intangible good which, none the less, if not taken up represents a very real loss of income to the industry. Travel agencies and airlines have a wide range of ploys to overcome these problems and to minimize such lost income. Discount arrangements, last-minute bargains and 'standby' fares are some of the tactics used to attract buyers when seats remain unsold. Conversely, ticket touts thrive when demand is greater than the number of opportunities available.

In the future, some schools and colleges might choose to market as aggressively as some tour operators in order to avoid lost income, now that a voucher system operates across most parts of the education service, and last-minute entrants carry with them as much money as those signing up months earlier. Advice given to those marketing tourism on publicizing spare capacity (e.g. Holloway and Plant, 1988) may be adaptable to the needs of education – another industry with a powerful seasonal pattern. The notion of a fixed price for a travel service has all but disappeared. Hotel receptionists are authorized to adjust prices for late arrivals, trade discounts within the industry are everywhere, prices fall out of season, and semi-legal organizations ('bucket shops') for the sale of cut-price air tickets have become legitimized. The expectation of lower than 'standard' prices is further encouraged by discounts for early holiday and air-flight bookings.

All this is not to suggest that the education service ought to emulate the tourism and travel industry. The industry also holds some warnings for other service industries of the dangers of a highly competitive market economy. Customers' tastes and preferences change, and the industry's market research is not always accurate enough to identify these shifts. Customers have also become accustomed to last-minute bargains, and so tend to make their holiday arrangements later and later. In consequence, the industry has become very unstable, leading to bankruptcies and bad publicity, thereby requiring an industry-wide insurance scheme organized through ABTA, the Association of British Travel Agents. The latter also provides a public relations function, which offers reassurance at times when public confidence in the industry is threatened. ABTA also establishes and enforces a 3000-word code of conduct on its members, and fines them heavily for breaches of the code. The value of a powerful national organization which speaks on behalf of the providers is a useful example for the education service. It supports those who have long argued for a General Teaching Council.

The banking service

Another service industry with possible lessons for the education service is banking. Like education, it has been criticized for being insensitive to the needs of its customers, and – also like education – the government has tried to deregulate the industry by encouraging new forms of competition from building societies and other financial organizations. In response to these threats, and to pressure from consumers, the provision of financial services has shifted from a provider-dominated industry to one much more responsive to the needs of customers. For example, a major criticism was directed at the very limited availability of banking services, confined to weekdays from 9.30 a.m. to 3.30 p.m. These are presently much more flexible, with opening hours having been extended and banks now open on Saturdays. Heavy investment in high-technology electronic systems has further extended basic services to make them available over 24 hours and 7 days a week.

Increased competition has led to massive advertising campaigns by all the major banks and many of their new competitors. Much of the advertising has drawn deliberate attention to the shift from a provider-dominated industry to one which is strongly customer-oriented. Advertisements have attempted to break down the image of the aloof, even hostile bank manager and replace it with an image of the friendly, instantly available and indispensable financial adviser. These developments are responses not so much to direct pressure from customers but rather to the findings of marketing research, which in all the major banks has been used heavily as an aid to management decision making, as is indicated below.

A number of lessons for the education service can be drawn from these striking changes in what used to be one of the most traditional sectors of the UK economy. One aspect of the banks' increased responsiveness to customer preferences in the face of increased competition has been the development of forms of non-contact services (banking's equivalent to distance learning). This comes from cash machines, computerized information systems providing statements and balances from high-street machines, and electronic point-of-sale payment services, as well as the 'First Direct' service referred to below.

The banks also demonstrate very obvious market segmentation, with aggressive competition for the student market accompanied by gifts and other inducements. In contrast, there is the equally determined but less obtrusive pursuit of the wealthier market segments, with the offer of differential interest rates, a wide array of sophisticated financial services and status symbol gold cards. These latter, along with decorative cheque books and cash cards, are attempts to provide some small tangible benefit to a service which in almost all respects is intangible.

Midland Bank provides good examples of this. Market research has identified groups of customers with different needs, comprising identifiable market segments. Three broad groups have been segmented mainly by economic status. Distinctive banking accounts have then been developed for each of these groups. The Vector, Orchard and Meridian multi-service accounts each offer packages geared to the economic circumstances of, respectively, young people with limited resources, better-off customers with savings and overdraft requirements, and the more well-to-do with higher overdraft limits, more interest on savings, gold cards and fringe benefits. More recently, the Bank has introduced 'First Direct' for those who do not want to use branches at all, but manage their financial affairs by telephone. There are further specialist services catering for the needs of small businesses and for corporate business customers.

The organization of the industry has changed, with marketing shifting to a central position. Midland Bank's marketing department includes responsibilities for strategic planning and internal communications, as well as the more immediately obvious marketing tasks. These latter are organized through three divisions: research and analysis, product development, and communications. The first of these is at the front end of the business, identifying changing customer expectations and needs and collecting intelligence from the Bank's branches. Intelligence is also gathered by thorough press scanning, by buying the results of omnibus surveys, and by carrying out some qualitative and quantitative research of its own. The product development section then responds to the findings of the researchers, developing new services, which are then test-marketed before being passed on to the communications section, who organize the 'launch' of a new service. The scale of the investment in research and analysis pays dividends by setting clear parameters for the work of the other two sections.

Midland Bank's marketing department employs about 200 staff, drawn mainly from the branches rather than bringing in marketing specialists. In-house sales training is another responsibility of the marketing department, and the company invests heavily in marketing to its own employees. All staff are trained in the skills needed for effective customer contact through face-to-face training undertaken in the branches and at local training centres. There is also a voluntary and comprehensive in-house distance learning facility, which provides knowledge of the company's products and awareness of its goals as well as support in enhancing individuals' personal effectiveness. The training schemes are complemented by incentive systems. Branch managers are rewarded for success – normally equated with exceeding performance targets in acquiring and retaining customers – with financial bonuses. Other staff who enhance their customer skills or otherwise improve their performance can receive gifts over and above the benefits built into the performance review scheme.

The Bank's investment in training for internal marketing is backed by investment in enhancing the quality of premises, with the removal of the forbidding security barriers and the establishment of a more welcoming environment designed 'to give the branch back to our customers'. These refurbished branches are characterized by readily available specialist services, including counselling, a 'Share Shop' and an 'Enterprise Centre' for small business customers. Staff help to project the corporate image by wearing the 'Midland Collection', a uniform designed for all staff dealing face-to-face with customers.

A large customer-oriented service organization such as Midland Bank has a number of features of interest to the education service. The centrality of the marketing function is one of them. The importance of marketing's location in the organizational structure is a major theme of Chapter 9. The emphasis on staff training, 'internal marketing' to the organization's own staff, and an incentive system based upon responsiveness to customers are also significant and are picked up in Chapter 8.

The scale of investment in marketing is also revealing. The Bank spends between £10 and £15 million a year on advertising alone, with of course further expenditure on other marketing activities. It has 6 million customers – so it spends at least £3 per customer a year on marketing. This is carefully managed centrally, with little or no discretion for local branches. Contrast this with the education service's absence of any central marketing effort and the dissipation of effort and budget among the nation's 30000 institutions. No-one knows how much is spent by the education service on marketing, but there are at least 15 million current customers: if only £3 per head were spent on marketing it would amount to £45 million! Only a few pence per year per customer would be sufficient to mount a very substantial national marketing initiative for the service.

Customer contact in service industries

A distinctive feature of service industries is their dependence on the staff who deliver that service, to a degree not normally associated with the manufacture of products. The service to a very real extent *is* the people who deliver it. Research suggests that on average some 90% of a service organization's staff come into contact with customers, compared with only 10% of a manufacturing organization's staff. And the specialist marketing and sales staff are among those least likely to come into direct contact with customers.

The marketing of tourism and banking both demonstrate the importance of people. In both industries, staff are recruited primarily for technical or administrative skills rather than customer contact skills. In organizations in which employees are likely to be in contact with customers more than they are with the organization's own management, there is a further possibility that employees associate so closely with the customers that they do not feel responsible for shortcomings and complaints, but agree with customers that problems are the fault of 'the management'. These problems are accentuated when segmentation of duties means that staff take responsibility for only one part of the service. Customer complaints can then be related to other staff with responsibility for a different aspect of the service package. Service industries need both organizational structures and staff motivation policies which ensure that, for example, a travel agent's representative is concerned with every aspect of a package holiday being sold, and not just the air travel part of it.

Employers, therefore, have to invest in strategies which ensure that these vital aspects of customer contact are handled well. This requires heavy investment in training employees in appropriate patterns of behaviour and the relevant interpersonal skills. Involvement with the organization's corporate goals and immediate targets is essential, and needs to be imbued through forms of staff development. Training and other forms of development need to be backed by incentives to motivate staff, as were indicated in the banking example above. Hotels go further. They commonly identify, reward and inform customers of their 'employees of the month'. Distinctive staff reward structures in the form of exotic holidays and no- or low-interest loans offer further motivation to employees.

Codes of conduct attempt to provide substitutes for the quality control mechanisms used on assembly lines. These specify both how employees in the industries should behave and how customers should be treated. The processes of customer contact and customer care are rationalized in both industries. Both invest heavily in computerized technology to improve their service and simplify contact for customers, through automatic teller machines in banking, and through viewdata booking systems and package arrangements in tourism.

Beyond this, organizational structures are needed which both involve staff in as many aspects of service delivery as possible and use their contacts with customers as a source of marketing research. In the example of the Midland Bank, branch staff are encouraged to contact their marketing department when they spot new trends or changes in customer needs. Careful sampling techniques then enable the department to check out such trends with its own research. The travel industry uses questionnaires to customers, undertaken at times when customers have time on their hands, in order to inform its market research.

An important question in any service industry concerns the place of marketing in the organizational structure. In an organization wholly dependent upon the success of its marketing, the marketing function is the central management function. And where marketing *is* management, is there a place for specialist marketeers or a specialist marketing department? In this situation, a 'marketing strategy' and a corporate strategy are one and the same thing.

Public sector organizations as service industries

Tourism and banking are private sector industries, whose marketing successes are measured eventually by the extent to which they are able to anticipate, stimulate, regulate and satisfy customer requirements profitably. Public sector organizations are not yet measured in terms of their profitability. They are now exhorted – and even required – to apply the substitute of 'cost-effectiveness' in place of profitability. There is at present a considerable – and so far not obviously successful – search for some equivalent to profitability in terms of 'performance indicators' (e.g. Chartered Institute of Public Finance and Accountancy, 1988). This approach does not tackle some deep-rooted problems which characterize many public sector organizations, because in exploiting the lack of a profit/loss measure in the public sector, it does not focus primarily on the quality of service. There are signs that this is recognized. In July 1990, central government launched a major 'customer service' initiative throughout the Civil Service designed not only to improve contact with customers but to emphasize the notion that 'colleagues are customers too'. Similar initiatives have been tried in some local authorities and in the National Health Service (NHS).

It is no easy task to inject such a marketing orientation into public sector organizations. While they are as heavily dependent upon the commitment and competence of employees as other service industries, there is not necessarily a clear recognition of this, particularly where the customer is not paying directly for a service. The providers of a locally or centrally funded government service do not necessarily recognize those with whom they are in contact as 'customers' at all, but only as the beneficiaries of some free or subsidized service – a view not shared by the tax-paying customer!

Furthermore, the delivery of services in many public service organizations, including education, is largely undertaken by 'professional' staff, with a commitment to a professional ethic which might not necessarily coincide with the values and objectives of the service organization. This is seen in schools and colleges where some teachers' first allegiance is to their subject area, rather than to individual student needs, and most markedly in higher education, where the research interests of individual staff might have little relationship to institutional objectives. Educational organizations need both to recognize the legitimacy of such perspectives, and to seek ways of reconciling them with the needs of their customers and the agreed institutional goals.

A marketing perspective can assist this process, by developing and using measures of customer satisfaction, and by developing 'internal marketing' strategies which both inform and persuade staff of the need to reconcile individual and organizational goals. The Responsive College Programme at the Further Education Staff College has developed and piloted several relatively simple instruments for gauging levels of further education student and employer satisfaction and for marketing to staff (Theodossin, 1989). These are considered in detail in later chapters.

Public sector organizations do not normally have the simple measure of profitability by which they can measure their successes. Customer satisfaction levels can provide one surrogate measure by which they might evaluate their effectiveness. They offer useful and relatively easily collected evidence of the service's responsiveness to its customers. Such measures are not sufficient in themselves. The purposes for which public sector institutions such as schools and colleges were established go beyond mere customer satisfaction. Otherwise, the original mission becomes perverted, as is the case with those exclusive private schools first established to make provision for the children of the poor. Public sector service organizations have public service duties and responsibilities, which are likely to expect them to reach out to those potential customers which existing provision fails to reach. They also need to provide services which go beyond satisfying customers' wants, and tackle real needs which might not be appreciated by those customers. The following chapters take this public service perspective, and look at ways in which educational marketing might go beyond the search for new ways of keeping its customers happy.

3 | Essentials of educational marketing

This chapter focuses specifically upon the marketing of educational services. It starts by describing a perspective or attitude of mind with which to view marketing activity. It goes on to spell out some key marketing ideas and concepts, which can be employed usefully in the marketing of educational services, and demonstrates the key stages needed in developing a marketing strategy. These are then related to the other central tasks involved in the management of educational institutions of every size or sector – staff management, curriculum management and resource management.

Marketing is an important management function, in education as elsewhere. It is closely related to the other key functions of an educational organization – personnel, curriculum and resource management. This relationship is explored in some detail in the latter part of this chapter. A central concern throughout this book is the exploration of ways in which the distinctive characteristics of education and its management might contribute to an approach to marketing native to the education service. Such an approach builds upon the strengths and traditions of the education service, and should disarm critics of marketing who accuse it of polluting education with alien commercial ideas and strategies incompatible with the fundamental objectives of an education service.

A marketing perspective

Education is a service, as the previous chapter emphasizes, with much in common with other services. In successful service organizations, a distinctive marketing orientation is readily identifiable. It is based upon attitudes, backed by activities, which give pre-eminence to the organization's customers. These attitudes are reflected in the way in which the enterprise is organized and managed.

A marketing orientation in an educational organization is, therefore, one in which the interests and needs of the pupil or student as customer are central. Other clients – notably employers and parents – are also recognized, and due attention is given to their concerns and needs. These needs are regarded as the central reason for the organization's existence, and are recognized as even more important than the needs of the enterprise's staff or owners.

Such a marketing perspective focuses upon *customers* and *services*. A framework for such a perspective can be seen in Table 1. It is largely but not only concerned about customer satisfaction. An educational marketing perspective is also concerned with ways in which existing services might be offered to new market segments, and particularly to those potential customers with traditionally low involvement in education. It seeks ways of anticipating the changing needs of its customers and of developing new services which meet those needs. It looks to ways in which its resources might be used to provide quite new kinds of services to new groups of users.

Table 1   A framework for examining the market

	Existing services	*New services*
Existing customers	Improving quality of current courses	New courses for existing groups
New customers	Market expansion: increasing participation	Diversification: new activities

A marketing perspective is also concerned with enhancing the corporate image of the organization and of the service generally. A concern for customer satisfaction includes the encouragement and promotion of the view that educational provision is a matter not just of current consumption – a major component of user satisfaction – but is also an investment in the future.

These attitudes are translated into action through the activities and behaviour of the organization's employees. These activities focus upon the customer, and include the initial quest for customers and identification of their needs, through to the delivery of quality services and on to investigations as to whether needs have been met and customers are in consequence satisfied.

This is achieved with the help of appropriate organization and management. The organizational structures are designed around customers and their needs, rather than on sub-divisions representing factional interests and staff wishes. The management processes focus on the delivery of quality services, and emphasize the provision of those rewards and controls which ensure that attention is concentrated on service delivery as efficiently and effectively as possible. In order to do this – usually with limited resources – these management processes need to integrate resources, staff capabilities and customer needs in ways which use minimal resources for maximum effect. This is not going to happen just because of the charisma or intuition of the managers or the good intentions of the staff. Careful planning is needed to ensure that the organization's marketing, resource and curriculum objectives are achieved. Management needs to operate in the context of a carefully worked-through marketing plan.

In order to achieve planned outcomes, a number of specific techniques and tactics are needed. One element of the marketing plan should be the careful improvement of the organization's capacity to operate these techniques and undertake these tactics skilfully to the benefit of the customer. These elements of marketing are discussed in detail in later chapters.

Understanding the market

Before any marketing strategy or plan can be determined, knowledge of the market to be served is obviously essential. A simple framework such as that indicated in Table 1 provides a starting point. Its value is that it defines the 'market' in terms of both services and groups of customers – actual and potential. A market analysis must take into account the constraints upon the organization and, as was emphasized in Chapter 2, these are much greater in public sector organizations than in the private sector. Public sector schools and colleges are not free to offer services of their choice to customers of their choice; indeed, the introduction of a

National Curriculum has reduced this freedom for schools. Educational institutions were set up and funded for specific purposes involving customers specified commonly by age group, and often by ability and geographical location. However, an examination of the theoretical possibilities is a useful starting point from which then to draw the boundaries of external requirements – and then to examine carefully just how fixed and how flexible those boundaries might be.

A market analysis enables consideration of ways in which existing services and customers differ from those of competitor organizations. This requires an 'intelligence service', which can investigate not only customer needs but also ways in which they are met by competitors. It is only then that the school or college is in a position to determine whether and how it might best meet those needs.

An initial examination of the market raises questions about both services and customers. To answer these questions, more detailed information is needed. This comes into two broad categories: the need to analyse information already available, whether within or outside the institution; and information not as yet collected. In the first case, some ordering and analysis of existing information is required, involving a *marketing audit*. The quest for information not currently available requires the rather different approach of *marketing research*. Procedures for undertaking both of these activities are described in Chapter 5.

Information from the marketing audit and marketing research needs to be assembled and analysed so as to provide a basis for planning. It needs to be considered alongside the mission, goals and agreed objectives already established for the organization. Public sector organizations must include here those objectives set by central government nationally and by the local authority or other 'owners' locally.

A simple framework for the assembly and analysis of market information is the well-tried *SWOT Analysis*. Its title is taken from the capital letters of the four cells shown in Fig. 2. Analysis of the upper two cells is based upon the careful examination of the strengths and weaknesses of the institution. The lower two cells use evidence from the external environment in order to consider the opportunities and threats facing the institution. Evidence for the SWOT Analysis can be found in institutional files and records and through the experience and knowledge of staff and students.

Strengths	Weaknesses
Opportunities	Threats

Fig. 2   Framework for a SWOT Analysis.

Suggestions as to how such an analysis might be structured and used are made in Chapter 5.

Whatever the techniques used, the assembly and analysis of information is a central and essential basis for the planning process. The outcome should be a *marketing plan*. This lies at the heart of the effective organization of educational marketing. As schools and colleges move towards more formalized planning, the marketing plan is likely to form part of the broader institutional 'development plan' or 'corporate plan'. Until recently, the use of rather formalized approaches to planning was not widespread in educational organizations, but this has changed recently as colleges and schools have been required by the government to prepare such plans. Chapter 4 discusses the relationship between the marketing plan and other aspects of an institution's development plan. Detailed guidelines for the planning processes and their incorporation within the broader corporate plan (e.g. McDonald, 1989) generally posit a rational planning model, whose applicability in educational institutions has yet to be tested. Limitations of this approach, and some alternatives, are considered in Chapter 4.

The plan needs to take available information, ideas and policies and turn them into proposals for action. The classic structure for organizing such action in marketing is referred to as the *marketing mix*. This was developed from analysis of the marketing of manufacturing products (Borden, 1965), and has four components, the '4 Ps': *product*, *place*, *price* and *promotion*. These are the variables which can be controlled and adjusted by organizations in order to produce a blend which represents the organization's preferred marketing stance. This simple and powerful notion is central to most marketing textbooks and training programmes.

Research into its applicability to service industries has led to criticisms that it is too restrictive a framework in that context. In particular, it takes no account of the paramount importance of people and ambience in marketing services. To remedy this, Cowell (1984) suggests three more Ps – *people*, *process management* and *physical evidence*. The seven concepts are summarized in Table 2.

Table 2 The marketing mix: Manufacturing and service industry definitions.

Product	The goods or services being offered to the market
Place	The location and accessibility of the goods/ services
Price	The resources needed by customers to obtain the goods/services
Promotion	The activities communicating the benefits of the goods/services to potential customers
And, for service industries:	
People	Those involved in selling and performing the service, and the interaction of customers receiving the service
Cowell (1984) has identified two further elements in the 'mix':	
Process	The operational system by which delivery is organized
Physical evidence	The environment in which the service is delivered, and the goods which enable the service to be provided.

The case for including an extra 'people' element in planning for the marketing of service industries has already been made in Chapter 2. In educational institutions, these 'people' include not only the teachers and non-teaching staff but also the students. However, the two final elements in Table 2 seem to be an unnecessary complication. The 'physical evidence' can be accommodated by broadening the concept of place to include the ambience of service delivery and any physical items which go with the service. The management issues collected together under Cowell's notion of 'process' are of a different order than the other elements of the 'marketing mix' and require separate consideration when examining the organizational framework which most effectively supports a marketing perspective. Organization and management shape every aspect of marketing, and are so central to effective marketing that they cannot be dealt with separately as an extra element of the 'marketing mix'. This book uses, therefore, a basic '5 Ps' framework for the educational marketing mix, which provides the basis for the detailed examination of educational marketing strategies in Chapters 6, 7 and 8.

Central to the planning process and an integral element in the 'marketing mix' is the identification, development and promotion of a distinctive and consistent mission, spelled out in the institution's succinct 'mission statement'. This is reflected in the positive image of the educational organization promoted through its marketing. Marketing devices such as the use of a 'logo', school uniform or high standards of out-of-school behaviour all play their part in this. Careful public relations, including a well thought-out media relations strategy, also contribute. Heavy government expenditure on the image of the city technology colleges demonstrates what can be achieved with a lavish marketing budget and heavy investment in public relations.

Most educational organizations are nothing like as generously resourced, but imagination and effort can often overcome the resource constraints. Basic marketing principles are important here: identifying clearly the market segments, and their needs, and deciding which of those needs can be met, before preparing marketing strategies which integrate all elements of the marketing mix and project the messages to customers about their services available from and through the school or college. And ensuring that the messages going out from existing staff and students are positive, based upon their own satisfactory experiences as deliverers and recipients of the services provided. Of course, these messages must be backed by action back in the institution to ensure that public relations promises are borne out by the realities of the customers' educational experiences.

Marketing and staff management

Marketing is a central aspect of institutional management. If it is to be effective it must be closely integrated with the other elements of management – staff or personnel management, curriculum management and resource management. These relationships are now considered in turn.

The main elements of personnel management can all be shaped by a marketing perspective. Recruitment and pay systems might look for and reward marketing skills and attitudes. Staff development and appraisal systems might seek to develop and enhance those skills and attitudes. This argues that the marketing plans and strategies discussed above should be directed internally as much as externally – and the former so often requires even more hard work and creativity than the latter.

A marketing perspective is one which encourages all staff in educational establishments to recognize that they individually have marketing responsibilities. These include promoting the organization's image and monitoring customer satisfaction, as well as carrying out their central tasks in response to and designed around customer needs. Part of these responsibilities should include shaping customer perceptions so that they recognize and respond not only to the quality of the teaching, but also to the likely benefits arising from learning experiences. These benefits are both the immediate satisfactions of the teaching and learning being undertaken, and the longer-term satisfactions achieved only when the benefits of an investment in education are reaped – and this should be a life-long process.

Robinson and Long (1988) advocate 'internal marketing' as a distinctive requirement for service industries in general and educational marketing in particular. This is defined as selling the job to employees before an organization can sell its services to customers. Applying this notion to further education, Robinson and Long (1987) argue that 'good marketing practice = good teaching practice'. This is rather restrictive: a major aspect of customer satisfaction relates to the quality of the teaching, but customer satisfaction relates to more than teaching. Education can be – many will claim should be – learner-controlled. Distance learning, independent study and cooperative learning are among the devices for achieving this without the direct, face-to-face involvement of teachers.

An effective marketing strategy should seek to influence the social as well as the educational encounters at school or college. The activities of non-teaching staff can be as significant as those of the teachers, and the overall ambience of the institution is also important. A marketing perspective should heighten teaching and non-teaching staff awareness of their roles in marketing the school services from the office, reception desk, telephone switchboard and the caretaker's office, as well as from the classroom.

This requires investment in staff development and training. Overall, a major objective of any educational organization's marketing and staff development strategies should be to enhance the organization's responsiveness to its clients and potential clients. Marketing research is needed which examines carefully the significant points of contact between clients and the employees in educational institutions. Initial contacts with educational establishments are frequently fraught with problems. Contact with institutions by telephone, letter or face-to-face is unlikely to be as welcoming as a contact with a high-street travel agent. Despite the efforts of many further education colleges, their enrolment procedures can still resemble the supposed mating routines of some large and rare mammals – occurring annually, with maximum inconvenience and minimal pleasure to both parties. Low morale and lower pay can lead to telephone and reception desk responses which discourage recruitment, even to the extent of the receptionist advising a potential student to try the rival institution down the road!

Educational institutions need to shed the images of hostile secretaries, truculent caretakers and ignorant telephone receptionists, along with their jargon-ridden publicity and other communications materials. This can be achieved by investing in forms of staff training, whose starting point is awareness-raising. Despite the impact of falling rolls throughout the education service and the consequent threats to job security, teachers and non-teaching staff all too often do not perceive students and pupils as customers, whose patronage is needed if they are to hold on to their jobs. 'Front-of-house' training, whereby staff are helped to improve the quality of this initial contact with customers, is an important aspect of any institution's marketing planning. It needs to be augmented by strategies for improving the appearance of those places where customer contacts take place, and by a stronger emphasis in both spoken and written forms of information upon the potential benefits for clients. Useful lessons can be drawn from the better primary schools, which, despite severe resource constraints, have made great strides in recent years in improving the appearance of the environment, and in treating parents and pupils in more welcoming ways, including the effective involvement of parents in the educational process itself. Most observers agree that the quality of teaching and learning has also improved. Strategies for achieving just such improvements are a major theme in Chapter 6.

One controversial strategy for heightening staff responsiveness to their customers would be to reward staff for particular demonstrations of effective marketing. The culture of the education service would probably resist attempts to emulate hotels in identifying, rewarding and publicizing the 'employee of the month'. However, the greater financial freedom which most schools, colleges and higher education institutions now or will soon have under the financial delegation (local management of schools/ colleges) sections of the 1988 Education Reform Act, makes it possible for institutions to invest in imaginative forms of public and private recognition for those marketing activities which contribute to organizational survival and prosperity – and such activities must surely include particularly successful teaching. The gradual implementation of school and college appraisal schemes, in response to the stimulus of government-funded research projects and training opportunities, provides further opportunities for such appreciation of high-quality work. Customer satisfaction surveys could well contribute to that appraisal process, as could the marketing research technique of spending part of a day following a randomly selected pupil or class through the school's curriculum offerings.

Marketing and curriculum management   *all this*

Central to the marketing of any educational service must be a concern for the nature and the quality of the curriculum. An educational marketing strategy must, therefore, both take account of the curriculum and attempt to influence it. As indicated earlier (see Table 1), this requires attention to both the customers and the services offered. Marketing research can identify new curriculum needs, and ways in which the current curriculum provision should be improved. It should also identify 'market segments' which could and should benefit from forms of educational provision not currently available to them. The record of the education service in providing access for traditionally disdavantaged groups is improving. The 1981 Education Act drew attention to the nature and quality of educational provision needed for those students – up to one-fifth of the total – with special needs, and it provided a framework for the improvement of that provision. Despite very limited resources for this purpose, schools and colleges have accepted that the education of students with special needs should, wherever possible, be integrated with that of their fellow students. Teachers and others have tried hard to recognize the needs of these groups of customers, and have tailored not only the curriculum but the support systems and premises where possible to meet these needs.

Government funding has supported experiments in providing access courses in further and higher education, e.g. for women in science and technology and for groups from some ethnic minorities. However, the education service has often not sufficiently publicized such developments, to the detriment not only of the educational institution but also of potential customers who have remained ignorant of the opportunities available to them.

Teaching and learning processes are at least as important as the curriculum content to education's customers. Some institutions have specialized in distinctive choice opportunities for their students, such as the Polytechnic of East London's emphasis on independent study, Oxford Polytechnic's modular curriculum and the Open University's use of distance learning. The institutions mentioned have promoted the distinctive nature of their curricula as part of their marketing strategies.

Schools and colleges could well benefit from a closer examination from a marketing perspective of the curriculum choices available to their students, including the teaching and learning processes they are expected to undertake. Thomas (1986) is just one of a number of critics of the limited choice opportunities in secondary schools, contrasting these with those available in good primary schools. The standardization imposed by a National Curriculum might be countered by a stronger emphasis upon the quality of learning opportunities and the individualization of learning. In an increasingly competitive environment, schools and colleges will need to identify responses attractive to potential clients, which emphasize the quality of curriculum provision rather than any distinctive content. They need then to develop strategies for drawing customers' attention to this.

Assessment procedures are also important considerations when customers contemplate possible courses of study. Some potential students will be attracted by continuous assessment methods with no or few formal examinations: others will prefer the opposite. The development of 'competence-based' approaches in vocational education and training offer opportunities both for individualized assessment procedures and for assessment as a means for exemption from parts of an educational or training programme whose objectives have already been achieved by the learner. The assessment procedures for the National Curriculum (Task Group on Assessment and Testing, 1988), with the identification of a sequence of 'levels' through which pupils progress in each 'profile component', have the potential for similar emphasis upon individualized educational programmes in the school sectors. Individual action plans are used increasingly in both school and post-school sectors in order to tailor educational provision more precisely to the requirements of individual students. These are particularly valuable when that provision is obtained from more than one organization, as when a trainee's individual action plan involves learning both in the college and in the workplace.

Marketing and resource management   – all this

Marketing requires resources, but is also an essential means for acquiring resources. The 'marketing mix' approach assists with the examination of the deployment and redeployment of resources. It requires consideration of the relative investment in:

- promotional techniques, including publicity materials, media relations and advertising;
- the curriculum and teaching/learning strategies, and most importantly the benefits thus accrued – the 'product' (or service);
- the environment in which the service is delivered (the 'place');
- the 'price' asked of participants taking up these educational services including, for students outside public-sector schools, the fees and other expenses, as well as the opportunity costs to students choosing to buy education rather than spend their time and money elsewhere; and
- 'people' costs, including staff development, training, organization and motivation.

An educational marketing strategy should, therefore, carry a price tag. A marketing audit should identify current resource deployment, and research findings may well suggest ways in which the same resources might be deployed more effectively. The marketing plan can then indicate ways in which resources might be both allocated and mobilized, in order most effectively to achieve the institution's objectives.

A distinctive feature of the marketing function in the public sector is the expectation that it will generate new resources –

commonly in the form of direct involvement in fund-raising. Most education sectors are becoming increasingly adept at this, with some investing considerable resources, including staff time, and reaping substantial returns. Marketing posts in further and higher education commonly require the holders to work actively in acquiring the additional resources associated with industrial and commercial sponsorship, and British and European governmental funding, as well as income-generating activities such as short courses and consultancies. Schools are following along similar routes. These approaches and some of the techniques employed are examined in detail in Chapter 9.

Resource management and marketing are, in consequence, closely interrelated. An institutional resource management strategy needs to take heed both of the costs of marketing and of the income generation targets to be achieved through effective marketing. As with curriculum management and personnel management, the close integration of these aspects of institutional management points to the importance of leadership skills and organizational structures, which enable these management functions to work together to achieve the common ends defined by the institution's mission and objectives.

Essential to any understanding of educational marketing is the recognition that it is a significant, indeed central, management activity. It relates to and influences the other major elements of education management: staff management, curriculum management and resource management. The basic marketing notions of marketing planning, marketing audit and research, and the marketing mix can all contribute to a clearer understanding of the tasks needed in order to manage and market education effectively. The next six chapters look in turn at ways of achieving these tasks effectively. Planning (Chapter 4), marketing research and the marketing audit (Chapter 5), the marketing mix (Chapters 6, 7 and 8) and the organizational structures needed (Chapter 9) are each examined. The intention in each chapter is to identify ways in which marketing might most usefully contribute to the effective management of educational institutions, whatever their size or sector.

4 | Marketing policies and planning in the education service

In this chapter, the ideas and approaches to marketing planning and the development of marketing policies, outlined briefly in the previous chapter, are considered in more depth. A framework for preparing a marketing plan is examined. Before this, the factors influencing a shift to more formalized planning in UK educational establishments are examined, and the relationship between the marketing plan and other aspects of institutional planning considered. The problems of planning in a highly politicized environment are then examined, and some suggestions made as to 'non-rational' planning approaches needed in such circumstances. Finally, the qualities needed in those undertaking the planning and the place of planning in an institution's overall management are considered.

Most schools and colleges are now required or requested to produce formal plans. The planning process has become an important component of the management tasks of head teachers, principals and other managers in the education service. Its importance has been highlighted as schools and colleges attempt to schedule the implementation of a bewildering series of central government requirements, including staff training plans, school National Curriculum plans and schemes for the local management of schools and colleges. Managers recognize that the complexity and volume of these changes argue that they are better tackled comprehensively within one institutional plan.

The central purpose of such planning is to enable schools and colleges to meet the needs of their students and other customers, and the requirements of national and LEA legislation. All this is to be achieved as cost-effectively as possible, making the most efficient and effective use of the available resources. Until recently, many institutions got by largely on improvisation, within a very loose planning framework. This approach is unlikely to be possible, now that central government has taken upon itself the responsibility for planning a very large part of the education service. Central government policy initiatives require a school planning response – even when the intentions are to subvert and modify those aspects of central government policy which are perceived by governors and education managers to be not in the best interests of the customers. 'Ad hockery' is of little value in an increasingly tightly regulated education service.

Arrangements for staff development demonstrate this. Until recently, most teachers and lecturers took responsibility for their own professional development. Some chose a careerist route through an arduous series of award-bearing courses. Others found that the classroom presented its own challenges, and asked for no further stimulus. All this has changed. The government has prescribed that teachers *will* develop, whether they like it or not. In the school sectors, their conditions of service have been unilaterally changed to require that they attend a number of additional in-service education and training (INSET) days, where they must enhance their capabilities to meet government prescriptions for the National Curriculum and its accompanying testing/ assessment procedures. Lecturers in the post-school sectors retain rather more control over their development. But in both the school and further education sectors, funding is held back to fund this staff development, and must be spent according to priorities set by central government. Local authorities must specify in the form of a bid for resources to central government just how they will use these staff development funds, and most LEAs extend this process to their institutions, requiring of them a bid for resources in the form of an institutional development plan.

The imposition of a staff appraisal system for teachers in schools, colleges and polytechnics, although not compulsory at the time of writing, has already encouraged a greater specification of teachers' jobs, the targets therein to be achieved within a prescribed period of time, and the activities to be undertaken in order to achieve those targets. In short, staff development and appraisal have become much more formalized and have stimulated the application of quite formal planning frameworks. Their origin as staff INSET plans has, however, meant that, even where they have been extended to include curriculum planning (a requirement for schools of the National Curriculum) and resource planning, they have not necessarily included marketing planning. And where marketing plans have been included, this has often been as a bolted-on extra planning element rather than an integral part of the overall process. This is unfortunate. The next sections suggest how it might be remedied.

The shift of many governance responsibilities from LEAs to governing bodies emphasizes the importance of institution-based planning. The removal of detailed regulation at local authority level is driving institutions to develop their own procedures for strategic planning, and for monitoring and evaluating the implementation of those plans. Many governors come from work environments in which they are very familiar with the application of formalized corporate planning, and can contribute usefully to these processes. Furthermore, a carefully worked out plan, which has attracted the support of all staff (and not just teaching staff) as well as the governing body, is the best protection against the eruptions of the maverick governor who seeks to impose changes and new directions not necessarily in the interests of the institution and its customers.

The planning process

The processes whereby an institutional plan might be developed is outlined for the schools sectors in a recent DES (1990b) publication. These processes follow a well-tried and rational approach, which contains within it a number of inherent problems. The processes are outlined first, before the basic characteristics of a marketing plan are considered. Some of the problems and health warnings related to such rational planning are then explored, along with some alternative approaches.

The development of any institutional plan requires firm leadership and a commitment to a clearly articulated set of values which spell out the institutional 'mission'. It is helpful if that mission can be expressed clearly and succinctly in a short 'mission statement'. This, however, is easier said than done. Even in a small organization it is unlikely that all staff will be in agreement as to that mission. There is, however, little point in having a mission statement unless it is actively supported by all staff. After all, in a service industry it is through the contacts between staff and customers that the mission is demonstrated. Care, time and effort are needed in order to involve staff in defining (or redefining) the institution's mission and in obtaining the commitment of all staff to working towards its achievement. This requires that managers consult as widely as possible with staff, parents and pupils. Each establishment will determine for itself the feasible boundaries between such consultation and more participative negotiation over the mission statement and the consequent planning processes. An arbitrarily imposed plan is unlikely to win staff support, and a supportive and committed staff is essential if the plan is to be implemented successfully. In any service industry, the corporate plan will relate centrally to customers' needs, and it is the staff rather than the managers who are directly involved in satisfying those needs.

The elements of the plan will vary according to local circumstances, but in most institutions a comprehensive plan is likely to require the components indicated in Table 3. The simple framework indicated is far more difficult to use than the table might suggest. If this were not the case, institutions would have formalized their planning procedures in this way years ago. In order to develop an effective plan, institutions and colleges need to work their way through a series of stages, which should take place at times which fit most appropriately with the other cyclical activities of the academic year. Part of the planning process needs, therefore, to include the effective planning of institutional time. Planning is a resource-consuming activity, and the most expensive resource it uses is staff time. The processes also require a range of technical skills, and institutions cannot assume that these will readily be found within the institution. It is necessary, therefore, to find ways in which these skills can be identified and then developed and enhanced through forms of development and training – another call on limited resources.

The use of a logical and ordered planning framework, time-tabled conveniently into the annual academic cycle of activities, is particularly necessary in a service with a series of externally imposed deadlines: the financial year; the different academic year and examination calendar; and the rather rigid deadlines for staff resignations and appointments. A further precondition for effec-

Table 3 Basic elements of an institutional plan for an educational organization

---

1. *Mission statement and objectives*: what the institution is trying to do and where it is going

2. *Situational analysis*: Statement of the current situation, spelling out the current strengths and weaknesses of the institution internally, and the opportunties and threats externally, together with the extent to which the institution is achieving its agreed objectives

3. *Planning elements*:
   - Resources: annual budget – income and expenditure forecasts related to previous year; premises plan; capital expenditure programme.
   - Curriculum: plans for reviewing current course provision; and implementing and supporting new courses
   - Staff deployment and training: staffing plan, including deployment, succession and other personnel management elements; staff development and training plan
   - Marketing: marketing plan with objectives, SWOT analysis, marketing mix and strategies

4. *Management and organization*: Management responsibilities/ deployment and changes; operation of planning systems; internal structures and their links with other organizations (including business and community). Organizational structures

5. *Monitoring and evaluation*: Financial controls; performance indicators and their uses; reporting procedures to governing body and externally (including LEA/DES where appropriate); teacher appraisal and student assessment systems; staff and student (and employers/parents where appropriate) evaluation procedures

---

tive planning is the organization of the institution's information in order that full use can be made of all the available information within and around the institution. One way of structuring the stages of planning is indicated in Table 4. As indicated, planning is not a distinct and isolated activity, but is part of a series of activities dedicated to the continuous improvement of the organization. These come together in a cyclical process, locked into the other institutional cycles. Thus in looking both backwards and forwards, the evaluation stage guides and shapes a rolling programme extending forwards for more than one academic year, so that this stage becomes the next year's review stage.

Table 4   The stages of planning

Stage 1: Review – 'What have we done so far?'

Planning starts with some review of what has been done so far, and what needs to be done next. A critical look can thus be taken at current targets and intentions, and the extent to which they are being achieved

Stage 2: Analysis – 'How well do we think we are doing?'

At this stage, the outcomes from the review processes should be considered alongside agreed institutional policies, LEA and national policy requirements and other initiatives, and an assessment of the institution's capabilities

Stage 3: Planning – 'What should we do next, how and when?'

The intention should be to produce a valuable working document essential to the effective operation of the organization.

Stage 4: Implementation/monitoring – 'Are we doing what we agreed to do?'

The plan will normally include an action sheet, which spells out who should do what by when, and provides a means for checking whether the agreed plan is being implemented as agreed. It should also spell out whose responsibility it is to undertake this monitoring.

Stage 5: Evaluation – 'Have we achieved our objectives?' and 'What should we do next?'

This is an ongoing activity, but is likely to be focused towards specific requirements, such as:

- the annual Governors' Report
- the annual LEA and DES planning requirements
- the annual budget and quarterly reviews
- the annual National Curriculum development plans
- the preparation of the next year's plan

The initial review stage involves the comprehensive examination of the organization and its environment which can be analysed by means of an *audit*, augmented by *marketing research*. The processes by which these might be undertaken are addressed in the next chapter. Some institutions may choose to include these processes within the general institutional planning procedures. Other institutions – and particularly larger ones – may prefer to undertake a distinctive and separate process of marketing planning, leading to a marketing plan which goes alongside the staffing plan, financial plan, curriculum plan, premises plan, etc., as elements of the institution's corporate plan.

Table 5   Framework for a marketing plan

1. Executive summary and action sheet

2. Situation analysis:
   - Internal profile
   - External environment
   - Resource audit
   - Current strategies
   emphasizing: (a) key threats and opportunities, (b) market segmentation and (c) course and other services portfolio and life-cycles

3. Objectives and targets:
   - Mission statement
   - Agreed/projected future routes and destinations
   - Objectives for selected market segments

4. Marketing strategies:
   - Target markets: trends, segment characteristics
   - Marketing mix: product, place, price, promotion, people
   - Resource implications, including income or surplus income targets; staffing requirements
   - Organizational implications, including responsibilities, deadlines and delivery structures

5. Action programmes:
   - Tactics
     - what is to be done?
     - by whom – responsible to whom?
     - by when?
     - using what resources? including staff, budgets
     - what promotional materials/campaigns?
   - Evaluation and review
     - performance indicators
     - marketing research facilities and related resources
     - tactics for steering action programmes, including contingency plans

Table 5 indicates a framework for a marketing plan. The elements of the plan are considered in detail in later chapters. It is offered as a checklist for the organization of marketing plans rather than as a template. Institutions will develop the planning structures which meet their particular needs, and with which those managing the plan will feel most comfortable. The degree of detail and specification will be shaped by the organizational culture, one dimension of which is the extent to which the organization operates bureaucratically, with fully documented and carefully specified procedures, or more instinctively, with back-of-an-envelope plans. McDonald (1989), in looking at the marketing planning of commercial organizations, could find no correlation between meticulously detailed marketing plans and marketing success. The basic principles are clear, however. Plans need to specify clearly the current situation, using research where necessary to clarify this. Objectives are then related to the current situation in order to define selected *strategies*, and then the more detailed *tactics* by which they will be implemented and controlled.

Forecasting and non-rational planning

The above sections describe and propose a structured and rational approach to the organization of an institution's planning processes. As was indicated from McDonald's research, this does not necessarily guarantee marketing success. A further problem for public sector organizations is that such rational approaches to planning, as advocated in the textbooks, show few signs of working in systems where 'pure' market forces are not allowed to operate, such as public sector education.

Educational planning has a very poor track record, largely due to the use of inappropriate 'rational' planning models, which fail to take account of some fundamental characteristics of the educational environment. 'Non-rational' or political models, which heed the confusion and conflict endemic in educational environments, have greater credence in a sector of the public service where political activity is unusually intense. It is ironic that, despite central government rhetoric over the past decade, the major interference with both rational planning approaches and the operation of a market economy is by the government itself. A highly interventionist approach in all sectors of the education service has negated attempts at medium- and long-term planning. At the same time, it has constrained the development of a free market in educational services. Too many variables are determined by government policies, and these change in response to political rather than educational requirements. Over the past decade, government interference has been extended into the school curriculum, the conditions of service of teachers, the total numbers and funding of students in higher education, and the provision of loans for students. The resources available for particular educational activities are much more closely controlled by central government than has been the case for many years.

All this is compounded by continuing and unpredictable interference with the local government sector, making the relationship between most educational institutions and the local authority 'owners' even more problematic – particularly when provision is made for institutions to change their owners and leave LEA control.

In this situation, the most effective planning technique may well be the ability to predict accurately the government's latest policy shifts. 'Non-rational' planning techniques such as scenario building (see Table 6) and the Delphi method (Table 7) are often as useful as the planning approaches outlined earlier. The future is an 'ill-structured problem', so that rigorous and 'rational' modes of investigation are not necessarily appropriate. Intuition and the 'art of conjecture' are high premium qualities. The improvement of predictive competence can be approached through the practice of intuition, instinct and imagination. Techniques for this can include 'mind-games', creative thinking strategies, role play and the generation and analysis of scenarios.

Tables 6 and 7 indicate two techniques which can be employed to structure the perceptions and forecasts of those sufficiently informed to contribute to this approach to planning. The techniques

Table 6   Planning through scenario building

Scenario building draws upon participants' imaginative and creative powers, in order to predict a range of possible futures:

Stage 1: Bring together a group of 'experts'. Generate a number of predictions and ask individuals to put three or four of them together; and then build up a scenario of the impact of these should they all occur within a given period of time

Stage 2: Scenarios reported to full group, who assemble them one on the other. Group either selects the perceived likelier option or establishes alternative scenarios where clear incompatibilities occur

Stage 3: The completed scenario(s) examined, and refined where necessary, then 'back-tracked' from the given date to the present time, to indicate events in sequence which would produce the scenario. The planning requirements of such a sequence of events can then be calculated

stand or fall on the quality of those invited to participate. The perception of customers is at least as important as that of 'providers' (teachers and managers) and 'owners' (governors and local and central government staff).

Table 7　Planning using Delphi forecasting

The Delphi approach draws upon the expertise of a carefully selected range of experts, and can be applied at a distance (by mail or telephone), to obviate the problems of bringing together busy people:

Stage 1:　Key issue requiring prediction identified, and key questions about this area formulated: questions piloted to clarify

Stage 2:　Panel of 'experts'/ oracles sent the key questions, and their replies collated into a consolidated list

Stage 3:　Consolidated list sent to panel members, who then rank the responses in terms of likelihood/ importance, etc.

Stage 4:　Responses again consolidated, in ranked list from 'most important' to 'x most important'

Stage 5:　Panel members asked to reflect upon differences between their personal rankings and the consolidated list

Power, politics and planning

A number of other analytical tools are needed to complement the forecasting techniques indicated above. These include the analysis of the institution and its environment in political terms, using a political analysis based upon the identification of power resources. Taxonomies of power such as those summarized by Handy (1986) can be useful here. These differentiate between:

- *position* or *legitimate* power, achieved by virtue of the position held;
- *expert* power, achieved by one's undisputed expertise or indispensability;
- *personal* or *referent* power, achieved through popularity or charisma;
- *resource* power, based on the capacity to reward or punish by giving or withholding resources; and
- *physical* power, based upon the ability to coerce others.

Power in this sense is the ability to make others act in ways they would not otherwise choose to act by virtue of one's position, expert knowledge, popularity, resources or threats, according to the sources of power held. Each source of power is manifested through distinctive methods, used to obtain appropriate actions or patterns of behaviour. Those with position power are able to exercise their influence through the manipulation of rules and bureaucratic procedures, which are accepted because of the authority of the power holder's position in the bureaucratic system. Resource power is exercised through exchange processes, whereby the power holder offers resources in exchange for compliance with his or her wishes. Expert power is exercised similarly, so that the power holder provides expertise or information in return for compliance. Persuasion can also be used by those with expert power, and is the method commonly associated with personal power. Physical power is, of course, demonstrated through the threat or exercise of force.

Such analyses enable those with planning responsibilities to assess both the sources of power held by individuals and groups influential within organizations and the methods by which they are likely to exercise that power. Assessment can then be made of the probable outcomes of current and potential conflicts, and of the strength and direction of recognizable trends. Planners can then examine the likelihood that particular plans will be supported or resisted by those individuals and groups, in pursuit of either overt or covert objectives. The planning process thus becomes the 'art of the possible' – the assessment of strategies and tactics which will win sufficient support to succeed. This involves the analysis not only of potential resistance by identified groups, but the possible coalitions which might form to resist the implementation of a plan. Planning goes further, then, by looking for ways to win over potential opponents and to weaken or prevent the formation of such coalitions.

In planning marketing strategies, such political analyses are valuable in assessing whether those with responsibility for implementing the marketing plans are likely to obtain sufficient support to be able to do so. They are even more important in a strongly politicized environment in estimating the impact and unintended consequences of particular strategies. For example, a further education college, when planning a campaign to recruit students from local secondary schools with sixth forms, may need to assess the power of the secondary head teachers and governors in constraining actions perceived to threaten the existence of those sixth forms – and the possible consequences of head teachers acting together within the local political system.

Planning skills

In practice, both rational and non-rational approaches to marketing planning are needed. The rational approaches indicated above
offer, at the very least, a framework and a checklist, by which
marketing planners might organize their activities and ensure that
important aspects have not been omitted. The political or non-
rational approaches are important in order to remind managers
that they are not operating in a 'perfect' market environment, but
that they need both to understand the political worlds in which
they operate and to have the skills necessary to be able to act
effectively in those worlds.

   Relevant and operable planning models, effective forecasting
techniques, appropriate learning models, and political strategies
for influencing others to use and value educational services are all
part of the repertoire of the effective marketeer. Educational managers with marketing responsibilities need an extensive portfolio
of skills and techniques if they are to plan effectively. These
include:

- A knowledge of and the relevant skills in the main techniques of
  forecasting, both for predicting future needs and for estimating
  their impact on (and ways in which they might be met by) educational organizations.
- Recognition of the different futures perceived by employers,
  employees and customers in the education service; along with
  variations in perceptions relating to gender, race, culture and
  social class, and the consequences of such perceptions on demands for particular forms of educational provision.
- The ability to analyse an organization in political terms, identifying power and influence and the objectives of key political
  actors; together with the political skills needed to operate effectively in that environment, to obtain and exercise power and to
  influence others.
- Judgements and insights of sufficient quality to enable them to
  identify those predictions, forecasts, and perceptions which require anticipatory planning within the educational organization
  and its environment.

   All this points to the need for marketeers with more than technical competence. Effective marketing is a creative process, and its
planning must not stifle creativity. Furthermore, those involved in

this planning need a deep understanding of the education service and the world of its customers. The intrusion of marketing expertise from commercial and industrial environments is unlikely to be effective unless accompanied by the qualities and insights indicated above.

Nor should planning be looked upon as an end in itself. It is an integral part of institutional management, and must be seen as such. Management approaches which seek 'continuous improvement' and 'total quality management' incorporate planning as a central element of the approach – but no more than that. From a strategic perspective on marketing, planning is no more than one of a number of necessary activities, all operating together and informing each other. It has been convenient in this chapter to treat planning as a separate activity. The next chapters examine the other elements of a 'total marketing approach' separately. But this must not obscure the fact that they all come together in practice as a central institutional management activity. The institution's leadership and organizational structure should ensure that they are successfully integrated.

5 | Information for marketing: Market audit and marketing research

The activities needed in order to collect, analyse and make use of information form the theme of this chapter. The effectiveness of any marketing strategy is dependent upon the quality of the information on which it is based. This chapter looks at the types of information needed, and suggests ways in which the information might be found and collated. Instruments for collecting information and strategies for analysing the information so collected are then described, followed by a discussion of the ways in which this analysis contributes to the marketing planning processes. The chapter looks finally at the establishment and maintenance of a marketing information system to support decision making.

The chapter is based upon three basic notions. The first is that structured techniques are needed in order to dredge for and then sift through the information needed for marketing purposes. The second is that most of these techniques are familiar to, used in and indeed promoted by, educational institutions. The third is that much of the information needed for marketing is already available in educational organizations, but its value is not necessarily appreciated. The chapter sets out, therefore, not to propose a series of approaches drawn from outside the education service, but instead to look at ways in which the service might adapt its own practices and use its existing data in order to inform marketing planning.

Educational organizations are awash with information. Filing cabinets, cupboards and computers are loaded with masses of information, mainly about customers. Further information is collected regularly for central government and LEA purposes. On the other hand, when marketing managers seek the information needed for developing marketing strategies and solving marketing problems, it is rarely available. The problems stem from the fact that information systems have been designed in order to *store* information, not to make it available for manipulation and analysis. Computer technology is now available in most institutions to facilitate such manipulation, but the intervention of people with both information needs and an understanding of how they might be met is needed if appropriate information systems are to be established.

Inadequate information was identified in a recent research study as the major problem faced by marketing managers in further education colleges (Gray and Williams, 1990), even though their institutions had invested heavily in a computerized management information system (MIS). In other words, the information was there somewhere, but could not readily be pulled out in a form useful for marketing purposes.

Marketing needs a marketing information system, and this does not need to be a system separate from other information systems in the institution. It should form part of the institution's MIS. Unfortunately, these systems are usually established for purposes other than marketing. Administrative officers set up information systems in order to track student examination records and whether student fees have been paid. Finance officers have them modified to ensure that goods are delivered and invoices paid. Marketing officers need student records and financial information. But they need the information both for different purposes and organized rather differently than do their colleagues.

A starting point then is some examination of the categories of information needed in order to undertake educational marketing effectively. Three broad categories can be identified. Information is needed about:

- the market outside the institution, including potential customers and competitors, and new needs;
- the extent to which current provision is taken up, and the levels of success achieved by those taking up this provision;

- the capabilities of the institution to deliver existing and new services; and
- the perceptions of current and former customers and their sponsors about the quality of service provided and the levels of satisfaction felt.

Much of this information is available, and needs to be organized in ways which meet marketing needs. The process of organizing and examining existing information is termed a *marketing audit*, and this is considered further in the next section. There is also information which is needed but is not available from existing sources. This needs to be collected, sorted and analysed. This requires *marketing research*. The two processes are examined in turn before ways of assembling, integrating and making use of the resultant evidence are considered.

Marketing audit

The notion of the 'audit' is derived from financial management but is just as applicable to marketing. Just as a financial audit looks hard at the existing information – the accounts, bills, invoices, etc. – in order to examine current practices and identify the current state of financial health, so the marketing audit seeks to understand the current situation with respect to the organization's marketing by examining in a structured way all available and relevant information. The structure is the key to this. McDonald (1989) makes the important distinction between those 'operational' variables over which an organization has complete control, and those 'environmental' variables over which the organization has no direct control. These are investigated by means, respectively, of an *internal audit* and an *external audit*.

The simplest form of audit, which brings together internal and external audits together in one analytical framework, is the 'SWOT analysis' described briefly in Chapter 3. Figure 3 spells out how this might be used to record those strengths and weaknesses identified through an internal audit, and the opportunities and threats perceived by means of an external audit. As much as possible of the information for such an analysis should come from firm data, but much will be 'soft' information, based on the observations, perceptions and estimations of staff and students. For this reason, it should be undertaken with a representative cross-section of informed people, including teaching and non-teaching staff and, wherever possible, students, who (at any age) have insights as customers which cannot be obtained from staff.

Some of the information needed for this can be drawn from institutional information systems, containing details of the geographical areas from which students are drawn (although this may need mapping from the records), variations in recruitment rates for specific courses and from different areas, and details of student success, failure and drop-out rates. Income and expenditure trends should also be available, along with relevant patterns of staff deployment (timetables). Records of student and community complaints may need to be extracted from a variety of different sources, but they should be available. There may well be forms of systematic institutional evaluation and/or staff appraisal or performance reviews, containing further relevant information. Marketing staff are likely to have to overcome problems of confidentiality when negotiating access to such information.

Strengths	Weaknesses
Record here the things which provide benefits to customers and staff in terms as specific as possible	Record here the things which the institution does not do very well, or which other institutions are better at
Opportunities	Threats
Record here changes which will increase demands for your services or encourage customers to be more successful or better satisfied	Record here trends or events which will reduce demands for your services, or which may lead to customers being more dissatisfied or less successful

Fig. 3   Using a SWOT analysis.

The information from these institutional records needs to be complemented by information from external sources. External visitors may have recorded their perceptions of particular aspects of institutional work. The trend is for increasing formality in these reports, as Her Majesty's Inspectors (HMIs) publish their findings, and local authority inspectors emulate HMIs by carrying out formal institutional inspections leading to formal reports. The validating bodies

Stage 1				
	Information required about current situation and recent changes and trends: What evidence is there?	Sources of information: Where can we find it?	Accessibility of information: How available is it?	Cost of information How expensive is it?
A. *School profile*				
A1. Mission/aims				
A2. Catchment area				
A3. Relationships with feeder schools				
A4. Relationships with next phase (schools, colleges, employers)				
A5. Course profile				
A6. Reputation				
A7. Self-image				
A8. Market position				
B. *School resources*				
B1. Teaching staff				
B2. Non-teaching staff				
B3. Premises: capital programme				
B4. Premises: maintenance programme				
B5. Student-related finances				
B6. Other formula-related finances				
B7. Other funds				
B8. Management resources (SMT strengths/weaknesses)				
B9. Organizational structures (strengths and weaknesses)				
C. *External environment*				
C1. Demographic trends				
C2. Political trends				
C3. Social trends				
C4. Economic trends				
C5. Market trends: market size				

C6. Market trends:
    customer needs/wants
C7. Market trends:
    new markets
C8. Competitors:
    location, market
    share and reputation
C9. Labour market trends:
    recruitment
C10. Labour market trends:
    student destinations

 D. *Current strategy and policies*
D1. Course development
D2. Other service development
D3. Marketing strategy:
    target markets
D4. Marketing strategy:
    marketing mix
D5. Financial strategy:
    student targets
D6. Financial targets:
    non-student-related income
D7. Staffing strategy:
    staffing changes
D8. Staffing strategy:
    management changes
D9. Staffing strategy:
    development/appraisal
D10. Organizational
    structure changes

Stage 2: Summarize the information from stage 1 in the matrix

	Information inaccessible but not costly	Information accessible but costly	Information inaccessible and costly	Recommen-dations
School profile				
Resource audit				
External environment				
Strategy and policies				

Fig. 4 What business are we in? A school marketing audit (adapted from Davies and Scribbins, 1985).

also undertake visits on which they report, whether these be the work of GCSE and BTEC moderators or CNAA institutional review panels.

In addition to this hard information, evidence can also be sought from what might be described as an institutional 'intelligence system'. This may make use of approaches whereby staff taste life as a student for a day, joining a class or going alongside a specific student and sampling the institution's offerings throughout the day. It may involve no more than the recent memories of students reporting on their efforts to enrol at the college, or of staff trying to contact colleagues back at school when working off-site. Developments outside the school may be known by students or their parents rather than staff, whether these are of new housing developments, skill shortages faced by a local employer, or of the changing reputation of the school in question or of a college in the next town. A device as simple as a SWOT analysis can extract this intelligence if undertaken with a suitably representative group.

The SWOT analysis is a simple but powerful framework for an institutional audit. At times rather more detailed analyses may be needed, which demand a rather more structured approach. One such structure is proposed in Fig. 4, which provides a set of questions to be addressed to a group of staff, students and governors, etc. The framework is organized in such a way as to draw the user's attention not only to some key questions about the information required for marketing purposes, but also to the efforts needed in order to obtain that information. It is, therefore, organized in two stages. Stage 1 requires the user to consider four aspects of the institution in turn – its profile, resources, external environment and current strategies and policies. Structured questions on each of these draw the user's attention to the information needs and to sources of information. The accessibility of such information and the costs involved in obtaining it must also be considered. When this stage is completed, stage 2 draws a summary of information in terms of both cost and accessibility, enabling recommendations to be made about the steps needed in order to acquire required information.

Marketing research

A rather different approach to the analysis of information bases the external audit upon the characteristics of the various market 'segments', and the internal audit upon the elements of the 'marketing mix', which are detailed in Chapters 6, 7 and 8. Thus information for the internal audit is collected about the *products* (services or courses, etc.), the *place* at which they are delivered, the *price* (and costs involved) paid for the services, the *promotion* methods used to attracts customers' attention, and the *people* who deliver the service.

For many if not most educational institutions, this form of analysis requires information not commonly to hand and available for audit. It is necessary to go out and collect this information, and marketing research is needed to do this.

The processes needed for research and investigation are familiar to all educational institutions. They form part of the services on offer from higher education institutions, and are used increasingly as part of the learning processes in every sector. It is not the purpose of this book, therefore, to offer guidance on conducting research. The principles, skills and techniques which characterize good educational and management research apply just as much to marketing research. If help is needed, Bell (1987), Powney and Watts (1987) and Bell *et al.* (1984) all spell out the principles and describe in some detail the techniques needed. This section concentrates instead on examining the questions likely to be faced by those who need to undertake marketing research. It focuses on ways in which the investigations might tackle three areas of research:

- researching the markets and their segments;
- examining aspects of institutional responsiveness such as customer satisfaction; and
- resolving specific marketing problems.

Few educational organizations have to hand information about the various market segments they serve in a readily structured or ordered format. It is necessary occasionally for marketeers to have to undertake a specific investigation in order to understand better the markets being served (and those markets not currently served, which the institution would like to penetrate). This can be approached in two ways. The first is through desk research, which examines information gathered by others about the markets. The second is through field research among the particular market segments about whom the institution wishes to find out more. But before market segments can be researched, they must first be identified.

Market segmentation

A 'market segment' is defined by McDonald (1989) as 'a group of actual or potential customers who can be expected to respond in approximately the same way to a given offer'. This is easy to state: it is a lot more difficult to specify in practical terms. A segment might be characterized in terms of age, sex, location, income, ethnic origins, religion, social class or employment – or any combination of these. Market researchers have also attempted to identify segments in terms of life-styles, values, personality and behaviour patterns. These latter require sophisticated and expensive analytical tools likely to be beyond the reach of educational market research; however, it might be possible to obtain access to such research which has been undertaken by others, and some sources are indicated below.

There are no obvious prescriptions for market analysis when looking at educational market segments. It all depends on the purpose of the market analysis. Thus school market segmentation may be defined mainly in geographical terms, as the distinctive characteristics of the different parts of a school's catchment area are identified. These commonly have an underlying socio-economic differentiation, as can be seen when schools describe their catchment areas when advertising for staff. However, Roman Catholic schools might find it useful to segment by parish, or to distinguish between Catholic and non-Catholic pupils. In some circumstances, differentiation by age group or gender may provide more significant market distinctions, as when examining the proportion of girls opting to study separate science subjects, or when schools seek to persuade 16-year-olds to remain at school rather than to go to college or to work.

Market segmentation is of crucial importance to the post-school markets. Further and higher education institutions have more flexibility than schools as to the range of courses to offer and the range of potential students to whom these might be offered. Marketing research is needed, therefore, first to identify segments large enough to justify a distinctive marketing strategy and, secondly, to determine the needs of this segment in order to examine whether the institution can meet those needs. If the answer is affirmative, the research can then provide a focus for service development and its marketing strategy.

In a further education college, the market segments are as likely to be defined in terms of age group as by geography, as the services for the 16–19 age group differ significantly from many of those provided in the same college for adult age groups. But more detailed sub-segmentation will probably be required, in order to provide information on which effective marketing strategies might be based. One such segmentation might distinguish between:

- *Individual customers*: divided into local and non-local, and 16–19 and post-19 age groups: the latter group might then be sub-divided into in-work and out-of-work segments, with further segments defined by gender, ethnic origin and special educational needs.
- *Corporate customers*: divided by size of organization, whether in private or public sector, and whether seeking consultancy or training services.

Both higher and further education colleges are interested in segmentation by nationality. Many institutions have now developed both sophisticated databases and distinctive marketing strategies targeted at specific segments in a target overseas country.

The processes of segmentation apply not only to individual potential and actual customers. Educational organizations may wish to segment businesses, using categories such as size, location, type of enterprise, or by the extent to which they undertake their own training. Businesses identified as not having an in-house training function then provide targets to whom college-provided training might be offered. Such segmentation also is valuable when undertaking fund raising or seeking sponsorship, as is discussed in Chapter 9.

As the preceding examples indicate, market segmentation is a creative process, whose purpose is first to decide whether an identified segment should be targeted, and then (if so) what strategies should be employed. This latter stage involves, as Table 8 indicates, the identification both of the benefits sought by the market segment, involving research into the segment's characteristics, and an investigation of the institution's capacity to meet those needs. This leads in turn to the preparation of strategies whereby the benefits might be promoted, including the development of strategies for that promotion.

A key feature of a useful market segment is that it should be large enough to justify the effort involved in researching further and developing services and a marketing strategy for it. This

Table 8 Researching market segments

---

1. Identifying bases for categorizing a market into segments
2. Collecting information about a market and sorting it into recognizable segments
3. Selecting the segments most likely to offer marketing prospects: matching them to institutional capacity and mission
4. Researching the characteristics of the selected segments: identifying benefits sought
5. Identifying marketing strategies for bringing benefits to the selected segment(s)
6. Implementing and monitoring those strategies

---

notion of size will be influenced by the perceived centrality of the segment to the institution's mission; the costs involved in marketing research, planning and delivery; and the anticipated returns in terms of numbers recruited and returns generated.

Other important features are that the segments can be readily identified. The sophisticated taxonomies of consumer markets differentiated by life-style developed by US market researchers are of no use to educational institutions if they require hopelessly expensive analytical instruments in order to spot members of a particular segment. Cheaper and readily applied tools for segment identification are considered below. Other relevant characteristics when segmenting the market are that the segments must remain both accessible and in existence. The investment of a lot of time and energy in identifying small businesses was of no avail in an inner-London area where most such businesses either went out of existence or changed address within a year of locating them.

The evidence for market segmentation can be drawn from a wide range of sources. Within the institution, student records normally differentiate students by location, gender, entry qualifications and age. Libraries should be able to assist with the provision of information collected outside the institution. This includes census information, which is however a resource of dwindling value as time elapses after the data were collected. Local labour market information is available in most parts of the country collected by Department of Employment initiatives, 'local employer networks' and local government planning departments and economic development units, who have frequently not only collected relevant information but have undertaken their own analyses by market segments.

The importance of information about market segments for commercial marketing purposes has led to the collection and analysis of census and other data by commercial market research organizations – who then sell it at high prices. Sources include directories of published market research such as *Marketsearch*, the Employment Department's and local authority local labour market intelligence, and specific market reports such as are published by Mintel. There may be situations when it is worthwhile buying the information, but the expensive guides are usually available at public libraries or in specialist collections of industrial and employment information within local government planning departments and some university or polytechnic libraries. Hill (1990) provides a useful overview of such sources of secondary information.

Once segments have been identified, marketing research is likely to be needed in order to determine further characteristics of the segment and the needs and wants which might be met through educational provision. The following offers an example of how this might be undertaken:

Example 1:   Researching the adult education market

The Head of Adult Education in a London further education college, concerned at the lack of take-up by non-indigenous groups, segmented the market by nationality, and then undertook interviews with community leaders of each of the communities thereby identified. This led to further segmentation of some groups by gender, employment status, age or location. The investigation enabled him then to identify key needs as expressed for some of those segments. Discussions with colleagues enabled him to identify those needs which the college would be able to meet, which in turn led to the restructuring of the adult education provision. Some needs were specific to a particular community, e.g. adult Greek women, while others were identified as being shared by several ethnic groups. He was further able to identify those groups who would be unlikely to attend courses at the college but would attend in a different location, so arranged to deliver some courses in premises provided by the ethnic community for whom they were specially designed.

As example 1 indicates, this is likely to require the familiar research techniques of questionnaires and interviewing. Central to this in designing a research strategy is recognition of the basic marketing maxim that customers do not buy products, they buy benefits. This is expressed more dramatically in the familiar marketing dictum that customers are interested only in buying holes when they examine the products from a drill manufacturer. In the same way, potential students are not as interested in the detailed syllabus of a course as they are in the benefits to be obtained from the course, whether these be the immediate gratification of congenial company and an entertaining teacher or the longer-term benefits of access to a job, another educational institution or a pay rise if they complete the course successfully.

This vital aspect of consumer behaviour is explored in more detail in Chapter 6. At this point, it is enough to emphasize that marketing research must focus on the needs of potential customers and ways in which they might be met, by identifying the benefits expected when taking advantage of a school or college's offerings.

Research with staff and students

So far, research evidence from outside the institution has been examined. Marketing research is needed within the school or college as well, in order to obtain that information not otherwise available. This is likely to concern issues related to quality of provision and customer satisfaction. Educational institutions have improved their techniques for internal evaluation in recent years. The 'institutional evaluation' movement of the early 1980s provided the impetus for a number of initiatives, some of which have been described by Clift et al. (1987), while the Schools Council-initiated 'GRIDS' approach (McMahon et al., 1984a,b) is still used widely in schools as a vehicle for collecting and analysing teacher and governor perceptions. These approaches have not necessarily led directly to the use of such techniques for marketing purposes, although there is no doubt that the focus on self-evaluation has created a climate in which issues of customer satisfaction and responsiveness can more readily be explored in schools and colleges.

The use of structured approaches for the examination of staff perspectives has become more common as a result of the interest in self-evaluation. In consequence, there are a number of instruments and checklists, some designed by local authorities for school and college use, such as ILEA's pioneer 'Keeping the school/college under review' checklists developed in the 1970s, and the more recent instruments from the 'GRIDS' team. These can readily be adapted to research into staff (teaching and support staff) and governor views concerning levels of service and perceived quality. The most useful evidence on these matters must, however, come from the customers. Fortunately, there are also instruments available to help marketing research here.

Specific techniques for researching customer satisfaction were developed through the Responsive College Programme (Theodossin, 1989). This further education-focused research and development project designed and tested some simple structured questionnaires which are now widely adapted and used in the post-school sectors to sample student opinion, at the beginning of, during and at the end of their courses. The project also developed questionnaires for sampling employer opinions about the college and the experiences of employees sent to a college for training and education.

Organizing market research

Marketing research can be expensive. Institutions can call in consultants to undertake the research, but even if drawn from another educational organization, such as a college or polytechnic, they can still cost a lot. Institutions might make use of their own resources in order to reduce such costs. Ways in which this might be undertaken include staff development activities. In most institutions, staff seek to enhance their management skills, and this is frequently undertaken through structured programmes of management development, leading to masters or diploma qualifications. Institutional managers now find it more difficult under schemes of financial delegation to find funds for tuition fees and staff replacement costs. They need to be convinced that such a development programme is worthwhile. Increasingly, managers are asking that staff undertake specified investigations as a part of the project work which forms an integral element in almost all such programmes. It might be possible to specify that the research element should be marketing-related and even to go on to define the area of marketing research to be undertaken. In that way, not only will the research be undertaken at low cost to the institution, but the normal help available from the project supervisor should provide a form of consultancy to the individual and therefore the institution. At the same time, a member of staff is acquiring and enhancing valuable marketing skills.

Another strategy for low-cost marketing research is to use student help. Business studies courses in schools, colleges and polytechnics commonly contain a practical marketing research element. The institution itself provides a laboratory in which such research might usefully be undertaken. Even where such courses do not exist in an institution, it may well be possible to use the school's marketing problems as a vehicle for a student project.

Marketing information systems

Once information has been collected and sifted by market audit and marketing research strategies, it is important that it is organized in ways in which it is readily accessible to those needing to make use of it. This requires a marketing information system. Every organization will want to develop its own distinctive system. As was indicated earlier, institutional systems are unlikely to be free-standing, but are more usefully part of the institution's management information system. There are, however, some basic principles and ideas to be kept in mind when developing the marketing components of an MIS.

The first is that the institution has an 'intelligence system', which regularly feeds relevant information into the system. This may require no more than that managers and others have a facility by which the intelligence gleaned daily – whether by reading the newspapers, talking with students and listening to gossip – can be fed into the system.

The second is that the intelligence is sorted regularly, and stored in ways which make it readily available to decision makers. This might be a task for a school or college library, as the information-handling skills are those of the professional librarian.

The third is that the information collected for other purposes by the institution needs to be organized and made available in forms helpful to those making marketing decisions. It also needs to be used alongside the intelligence referred to above, so should be sorted in ways compatible with the ways in which intelligence is filed.

Fourthly, the information system should readily identify gaps in the system: information needed but not available by any of the normal collection methods. This provides a focus for targeted marketing research.

Finally, and most importantly, the marketing information system should inform those with curriculum development responsibilities, so that the course provision is tailored to market needs. The example of the Midland Bank in Chapter 3 demonstrates how the product development process is informed by the research and analysis group. In the education service, curriculum development has normally preceded marketing considerations. A marketing information system should enable institutions to reverse this.

Underlying all of the above is the principle that a marketing information system must assist and improve the marketing function. It must not become some kind of Frankenstein's monster which requires so much time and effort to maintain and make sense of that managers have no time to use it to market more effectively. This requires that the marketing users are involved in the design of the system: they are able not only to specify what information is most likely to be needed and in what formats, but also to judge the volume of information with which they are able to cope. The temptations for systems designers to develop elegant systems too sophisticated for their users must be resisted. Quick and cheap methods of information handling are all that education managers are likely to be able to use effectively.

6 | Marketing strategies: The educational 'marketing mix'

The elements of the marketing mix were outlined in Chapter 3, where five elements – product, place, price, promotion and people – were identified as a useful framework for developing educational marketing strategies. This chapter looks at the first three of these elements in turn, and considers ways in which they might be analysed by education managers in developing the appropriate marketing mix for their own institution. The next two chapters then examine promotion and people, before looking at the processes of blending the elements into a successful 'mix'.

Three distinct notions are central to the idea of the marketing mix. First, it is not enough to concentrate on producing a good product, or a high-quality service. That service must be developed with its market and the needs of its customers in mind right from the start of the development process and throughout its delivery and evaluation. The institution's costs in developing and delivering the service must be considered, along with all aspects of the price likely to be asked of customers. The views of those delivering and supporting the delivery must be listened to from the outset, and the methods for conveying information to potential customers must be borne in mind along with the location and accessibility of the institution.

A second basic principle about the marketing mix is that marketing involves a lot more than selling. Decisions about the ways in which a service is promoted are shaped by and consequent upon earlier decisions about the needs of the market and the characteristics of the service. Decisions about the range of courses and the quality of the curriculum are *marketing* decisions.

Thirdly, a successful marketing strategy needs to bear in mind each of the elements of the marketing mix, and recognize how they impact upon each other. It is the blend of elements which produces the successful mix, and the successful blend is not achieved through quantitative analysis. A 20 percent investment of resources and effort into each of the five elements is not likely to lead to a winning recipe. An appropriate strategy is based upon marketing research which provides information about each element of the marketing mix, including the resource capacity and academic and other capabilities within the organization. Although the elements are examined separately for convenience here (and in the marketing plan), in practice they are considered in relation to each other when planning effective marketing strategies.

Product   *all this*

This should, of course, read 'service', but that would spoil the symmetry of the '5 Ps' mnemonic. This heading covers the range of services provided by a school or college. These are, of course, primarily the courses on offer to students, but they extend beyond the curriculum. The services might range, according to the sector, from the extra-curricular computer club at a local primary school to a university's contract research programme, and from a further education college's provision of hairdressing and restaurant meals to the general public to a polytechnic management department's consultancy service to local businesses. Nearly all institutions also have to make decisions about their range of student or pastoral services and the ways in which they should be delivered. Issues raised in this section include the features of an institution's 'product mix' and techniques for analysing that mix. Issues of product delivery and of quality are also examined, and particular reference is made to the supplementary and non-educational services which augment the basic educational provision of a school or college.

All institutions have a 'product mix', and this is usually reviewed fairly regularly in order to determine whether the same broad mix should be continued, whether the institution has the capacity to continue to deliver as before, and whether to fine-tune by modifying the delivery of existing products. It is also the case that some courses are seen as more central to the institution's 'product mix' than others. The government has determined that mathematics, science and English are the most central or 'core' parts of the school curriculum. Local authorities have in the past determined that specified colleges will provide key courses such as catering, building or engineering and that other colleges will not offer those courses (although the authorities' power to determine this is more problematic now).

Analysing the educational product

In developing a 'product' strategy, a thorough analysis of con-straints from both a technical and a political perspective is necess-ary, before going on to identify ways of improving this vital aspect of an educational organization's marketing. One framework for such an analysis identifies a number of categories of *constraints*. Each can then be analysed in turn, as indicated below. An analysis of such constraints from the political perspective discussed in Chapter 4 should enable the marketing manager or team to iden-tify those constraints which might be challenged with appropriate strategies, and those which are so firmly implanted that any mar-keting strategy must work around them as 'givens'. Recommenda-tions can then be made as to the product strategy in the light of these constraints, including the distinction between those con-straints to be taken as 'givens' and those which the strategy should try to reduce, bypass or eradicate.

Five categories of constraints might be identified, although these will vary according to the institution being analysed. They are system constraints, funding constraints, personnel constraints, political constraints and demographic constraints:

1. *System constraints* include the time-scale for institutional, gov-ernmental (including LEA) and other responses to new initia-tives; and the curriculum and validation limitations imposed through a National Curriculum, together with the requirements of examination and validating bodies.
2. *Funding constraints* include restrictions on institutional control over its own finances, as when institutions are not allowed the flexibility of a one-line budget; the lower level of funding avail-able for some student groups and courses (such as those for part-time evening students in higher education); and restrictions on

fee income by fixing prices outside the institution and by claiming back all or part of any surplus income earned from self-financing activities. Other financial constraints include reduced levels of funding arising from central government policies, as when prices were fixed by The Training Agency for trainees on youth and adult employment programmes; and the lack of funds for up-to-date equipment, materials and textbooks.

3. *Personnel constraints* to be taken into account include the lack of flexibility for staff deployment arising from conditions of service, including the working day, week, year and patterns of teaching; and the availability of staff expertise, especially in subject areas where there are major national problems in attracting appropriately qualified staff, such as science, technology and mathematics. In turn, there are the problems of dependence on short-term, part-time contracted staff, and of motivating poorly paid staff with limited or non-existent career prospects – and that can apply to full-time permanent staff as well as the part-timers.

4. *Political constraints* include the efforts and demands of powerful groups within and outside the institution for particular forms of curriculum provision. This might be pressure by a community group for a specific form of religious education, the demands of a dominant head of department that additional resources be diverted into that department's coffers, or the refusal by some staff to undertake outreach work or to operate certain forms of student grouping, such as mixed-ability, mixed-age or ability-streamed groups.

5. *Demographic constraints* emphasize the need to focus more strongly upon services for non-traditional groups where the total numbers of traditional customers are declining or the socio-economic nature of those groups is changing. This leads to a review of recruitment and enrolment procedures, and of teaching and learning strategies, which may not be appropriate to the needs and expectations of new customers.

Recommendations concerning the development of the institution's 'product mix' can be derived from an analysis of the constraints and the application of marketing techniques, including marketing research and the product life-cycle and portfolio analysis approaches indicated below. The resultant strategies will include those designed primarily to reduce or eradicate unnecessary constraints as well as those whose purpose is to develop a course portfolio which matches as closely as possible the needs of the institution's customers.

Internal and external influences on product development

The basic service decisions made by educational organizations relate to the range of courses and programmes to be made available to its clients. To some degree – indeed, for UK schools to an increasing extent – these are predetermined by government diktat. The National Curriculum specifies the core and foundation subjects to be taught to young people from the age of 5–16. Even with these constraints, schools and their constituent departments need to make service decisions about the ways in which they will deliver those subjects, and about the range of curriculum provision outside the National Curriculum.

In post-school education, not even the universities are completely free to decide their 'product range'. The higher education funding bodies (the Polytechnics and Colleges Funding Council and the Universities Funding Committee) make some specification as to the courses which can be provided in return for the funds received. The approval of the major accreditation bodies in further and higher education, such as BTEC (the Business and Technical Education Council) and CNAA (the Council for National Academic Awards), is needed before award-bearing programmes can be launched. This provision is regularly reviewed and revalidated – although the initial decision to plan a course and seek validation remains with the institution, and the polytechnics and some large colleges have had delegated to them by CNAA the validation of their own courses. Central government has sensibly not interfered directly in these processes in post-school education, except in the field of initial teacher education – with consistently disastrous results.

There is limited scope, therefore, for adjusting institutional 'product ranges'. Further and adult education have the capacity to close down courses instantly as student numbers fall below previously established minimum levels. Schools are required to provide some optional or additional courses outside the National Curriculum, and the decision as to which courses to offer and whether or not to continue to offer them still rests mainly with the staff and the governing body. Schools also have a lot more flexibility with post-16 or sixth-form provision.

Until now, course development has been product-led rather than market-led. The availability of specific teachers has largely determined the options offered in the fourth year and the sixth form by many secondary schools. It has been fairly typical for higher education institutions to build courses around teacher preferences rather than customer needs, looking first at what the teaching staff would like to teach, and then designing a programme which matches their interests, as example 2 demonstrates.

Example 2: Course development, polytechnic style

A departmental team in an English polytechnic decided to develop a highly specialist masters' programme. They sat in meetings for week after week, unable to decide the themes and structures for the programme. They resolved their difficulties in the end by listing the specialist interests of each team member, dividing these into a series of 'components' and asking each small group thus identified to go away and write a syllabus of specified length. Customers were not even referred to, let alone involved.

Weaknesses of this provider-led approach have included an insufficiently clear recognition of market segments, the absence of systematically collected data relating to market needs, and inadequate links with those interested in student progress, such as parents and employers. The first and second of these problems were examined in Chapter 5, when considering marketing research strategies. The problem of inadequate links with parents and employers has been tackled by government intervention. This has been attempted in part by specifying a curriculum which is supposed to represent customer interests, and in part by restructuring governing bodies to include parents and business interests to represent consumer interests – and by increasing their powers to influence the curriculum. The funding and organization of training provision has also been handed over to employer-led bodies, the Training and Enterprise Councils. There is as yet little evidence one way or the other to indicate whether these changes have made school and college product ranges more responsive to customer needs.

Course life-cycles

A further weakness of a provider-led approach has been the absence of a recognizable and finite 'life-cycle'. It has been convenient, with limited resources for course development, to retain existing courses as long as possible. In this way, expensive investment in curriculum development – and possibly in new staff – can be avoided. Services, however, share with manufactured goods a limited shelf-life. No course lasts for ever. This concept of a *product life-cycle* is summarized in Fig. 5. It is commonplace in the manufacturing and marketing of products such as cars, soap powders and chocolate bars. However, it translates less obviously into educational terms. It can be seen in the Open University's course planning processes, where courses have a notional shelf-life, before coming up for renewal (although resource constraints can put back the redevelopment process). Higher education institutions outside the university sector have received approval from their validating bodies to deliver approved courses for a fixed period of time, with a notional 'course life' in mind, after which renewal or replacement is

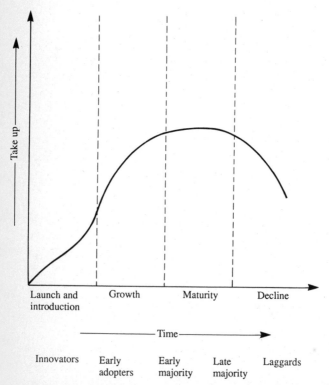

Fig. 5 The product life-cycle.

expected. Schools commonly plan their course development activities with notional 'life-cycles' in mind, as when primary schools phase their curriculum redevelopment strategies over several years, taking a subject area at a time.

Courses in every sector go through a development process in which the notion of the 'life-cycle' can assist in planning and in making marketing decisions. A new course normally requires substantial expenditure at the outset, on developing it, on informing customers of the course's availability and on training staff to deliver it effectively. The government's expenditure on both advertising literature and staff training for its National Curriculum is a good recent example of this. It is important that this expenditure is not judged only in relation to the initial take-up, but is seen rather as an investment in a longer-term process. It can take several years before a new course is well enough established to attract sufficient students to justify the initial development and promotional costs. In these early years protection may be needed from institutional policies which fix rigid criteria for course viability.

Courses then go through processes of growth and maturity. In the post-school sectors, new customers are likely to be attracted to a new course as messages of its availability and benefits spread through word-of-mouth and more structured publicity. Competitors may then be attracted to offer similar provision, so that take-up levels off in the period of maturity. Eventually, the course becomes so well-established that too many institutions offer it, or perceived benefits dwindle, particularly (as with a vocational course) those job opportunities requiring the new course are filled by those who completed it first, so that later students find it difficult to get work. Or fashions change and students no longer wish to train as mechanical engineers or obtain qualifications in Old Icelandic.

At that point, energy and morale are sapped in trying to maintain a moribund course, and the institution must decide whether to close the programme or to re-launch it with a revised curriculum and a new promotional campaign. The identification of recognizable life-cycles for an institution's or department's courses enables the time-consuming and expensive processes of course replacement or renewal to be scheduled, so that they do not all need to take place at the same time – a lesson recognized by the government in its schedule for phasing in the National Curriculum.

Course portfolios

A marketing perspective looks beyond individual courses or the offerings of one department, at the overall course provision of an institution. This *product mix* needs to be reviewed fairly regularly in order
to determine whether the same broad mix should be continued,
whether the institution has the capacity to continue to deliver as
before, and whether to fine-tune by modifying the delivery of existing
products. It is also the case that some courses are seen as more central
to the institution's mission – and therefore in its 'product mix' – than
others. Institutions need to review their course profiles regularly, and
to reflect upon the health, stage in the product life-cycle, and relative
significance to the institution of particular courses.

	High ———— Relative market share ———— Low	
High Market growth rate	Stars	Question marks
Low	Cash cows	Dogs

Fig. 6 The Boston matrix.

One device whereby the mix might be reviewed is that of *portfolio analysis*, developed from the initial simple matrix developed
by the Boston Consultancy Group and so known as the 'Boston
matrix'. This is illustrated in Fig. 6. It relates the proportion of
market share held by an organization's products to the growth rate
of that market. In this way, organizations can plan their marketing
and investment strategies. 'Cash cows' are steady revenue producers in areas where the product dominates a rather small market. 'Stars' require heavy investment in order to maintain
dominance in a growing market. 'Question marks' present problems – why is the market share so small, and should the producer
invest to increase sales or pull out of the market? 'Dogs' are only
worth maintaining if they produce revenue with relatively little
attention, or if they are 'jewels in the crown' of the organization,
important for promotional purposes.

The approach is so obviously geared to profit-seeking manufacturing organizations, that it does not translate readily to the needs

of many educational establishments. However, this basic approach has been elaborated, for example by McDonald (1989) and Kotler and Fox (1985). Some of their ideas have been adapted in order to develop a matrix for the analysis of educational services, as is indicated in Fig. 7, where it is demonstrated as applied to a poly-technic department's services.

The approach involves the identification of two distinctive service attributes:

1. *Market significance*, determined in terms of a service's *centrality* to the institution's mission and its *viability*.
2. *Competitive position*, as shaped by their perceived *quality* and their *accessibility*.

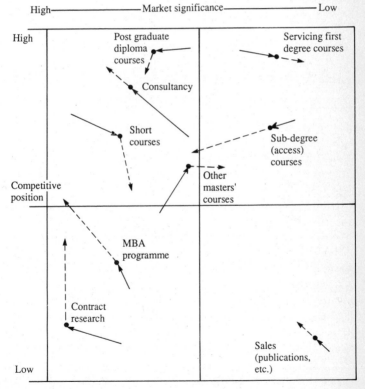

Fig. 7   Course portfolio matrix analysis, as applied to a polytechnic management department.

Key: position   ●————————▶ position
                2 years ago   present position   2 years hence

The matrix provides a means for demonstrating past changes and for anticipating shifts in the competitive position and significance of any individual course or other service, as is demonstrated in Fig. 7.

This approach requires means for analysing each of these attributes. *Market significance* is essentially an internal assessment. It reflects the relative significance of an institution's services, as perceived internally. A SWOT analysis provides some evidence for estimating significance, and it is possibly identifiable through an institution's mission statement and objectives. Centrality might in part be determined externally, as with the central significance of mathematics, English and science in the National Curriculum. It is demonstrated internally by the ways in which option choices are organized, departments or sections are staffed, and time is allocated to particular subject areas.

This is tempered by considerations of service viability. This involves internal management decisions concerning the minimum course size, below which provision will cease and students transferred either to another course or another institution. The protection given to some courses whose numbers fall below levels regarded as unviable elsewhere in the organization may be a demonstration of perceived market significance.

In contrast, *competitive position* is an external or customer assessment of a course's rating relative to provision in other institutions. Recruitment records of student take-up at similar institutions demonstrate their relative standing in the eyes of customers. External assessments of competitive position and perceived quality may be obtained from national league tables, drawn up by the educational press for teaching and research quality in higher education departments, based upon peer assessment. Higher education customers are advised by a growing number of consumer guides (e.g. Heap, annual) which provide annual ratings for colleges, polytechnics and universities and their constituent undergraduate courses. Government requirements for the publication of examination results were intended to provide similar assistance in making comparisons between secondary schools. Published HMI reports provide further occasional evidence of such external assessments of quality.

In using the course portfolio matrix, account should be taken of the 'life-cycle' of the services under consideration. In this way, courses which are well-established and central to an institution's mission can be revised and updated, in order to maintain their competitive position. Similarly, new services can be protected and promoted, in order to shift them over a period of years from a weak market position with low viability to a position where they are both important to the institution and in a strongly competitive position.

The portfolio analysis can be used in a variety of other ways. 'Market attractiveness' is related to 'business strengths' by McDonald (1989) in a matrix which facilitates the comparison of different products with a number of market segments, ranked in terms of their relative attractiveness to the organization. The approach can readily be adapted by educational organizations, who can relate their course profile to their different market segments in simple graphical form.

Influencing product decisions

Decisions concerning course development, expansion and closure are shaped by both internal and external forces. The external forces have grown in importance in the last decade, as the government has reshaped the school curriculum, and the national funding bodies have influenced higher education provision. The scope for internal influence has, therefore, been reduced, but by no means eliminated. Educational institutions are commonly highly politicized organizations, and it is likely that decisions concerning course expansion and closure will continue to be influenced by the internal political processes of bargaining, negotiation and conflict-management, rather than by any supposedly 'rational' use of analyses such as are demonstrated in Figs 6 and 7. Where such techniques are used, it is as likely to be in support of a political campaign as it is for use as a tool for rational decision making.

A marketing perspective can contribute to the processes of course development by emphasizing the evidence, from marketing audit and research, of trends in demand over time, of customer views from satisfaction surveys, and of the needs and wants of identified market segments. These arguments become more potent when they are costed, so that the resource implications of alternative patterns of provision can be examined.

Delivery and quality issues

Decisions about the nature of course delivery and the perc .eived quality of that delivery are as important as those concerning , course content. A customer-oriented philosophy, which argues that services should be delivered as though the provider was at the receiving end, is central to the marketing perspective. This should inform in particular those countless decisions in educational organizations about modes of course delivery, teaching and learning methods to be deployed, and the extent to which the course can be tailored to meet the needs of individual course members. Issues concerning the delivery by non-standard approaches such as distance learning are explored later in this chapter, when looking at the concept of 'place', but they form part of the 'product' decisions which derive from questions about the modes of learning most appropriate to particular groups of customers.

Underlying this viewpoint are the twin notions of 'entitlement' and 'quality'. The idea of a student being *entitled* to a service to at least a minimum standard is still unusual in English education. It has implications for the ways in which teachers prepare learning materials, the nature of the learning activities within and outside the classroom or workshop, and the extent to which these learning experiences are tailored to the needs of individuals, including those individuals identified as having special educational needs.

The notion of *quality* goes beyond this. Forms of 'quality control' which involve staff self-evaluation and the review of student satisfaction levels help to monitor whether previously agreed standards have been maintained. They do not compensate students when standards have slipped. Notions of 'excellence' and 'quality assurance' are more concerned with getting it right the first time, and of ensuring that the learning experiences, however organized, will be stimulating, exciting and geared to the needs of individuals.

The 'market-led curriculum' derives from such approaches. Teachers and managers have the difficult educational task of reconciling a curriculum which meets individual needs and expectations with the requirement to deliver a curriculum to internally and externally validated standards. The problems become more acute when the curriculum content is determined externally – which is why so many educationalists are so opposed to the traditional features of the school National Curriculum. However, when the same curriculum content is being delivered by all schools, it is the distinctiveness of the learning experiences which distinguishes one institution from another. The ability of teachers to design and deliver high-quality learning opportunities then become crucial.

Evaluation procedures can provide some evidence of this, but in any school or college there is no need for formal evaluation to identify those teachers and classes where learning is particularly exciting: word of mouth conveys these messages, both internally and externally, to potential customers.

The use of sensitive diagnostic assessment procedures can also contribute to that feeling of a high-quality curriculum which is meeting individuals' needs. Schools and colleges have made considerable progress in recent years in developing diagnostic continuous assessment strategies and individualized records of achievement. When combined with individual action plans, guiding students through modularized learning routes, these can further enhance the sense of satisfaction that the customers are receiving a high-quality, personalized service. This needs to be backed, however, by effective counselling and other support services, if the student experience is not to be fragmented, and this draws attention to the need for recruitment and staff development policies which reinforce the concepts of customer entitlement and the market-led curriculum.

Supplementary and non-educational services

So far, only courses have been considered, but educational services go well beyond the institution's formal curriculum. These additional services should not be seen as fringe or unimportant parts of the institution's offerings. They may be more important in attracting and retaining customers than the curriculum on offer. A distinction can be made between those *supplementary* services which support and augment the basic educational provision, and those which make use of institutional facilities for groups other than those using the basic services, including those for *non-educational* purposes.

The first category includes student support services such as careers advice, academic and personal counselling, and religious facilities. These are so integrally organized in primary and secondary schools that providers would probably object to their designation as 'supplementary' services, but perceive them rather as part of the basic or 'core' service of the institution.

Other support or supplementary services are more tangible. They include the provision of library services, facilities for food and drink and other purchases, and provision for recreation and sport (over and above the 'physical education' component of the school or college curriculum). They also include the materials given out as part of the curricular provision: stationery such as ring-binders, exercise books and writing materials. Some of these have so long formed a part of the basic provision by schools and colleges that it is difficult for some to recognize that they are not part of the basic educational service. An international perspective is needed to recognize that these are not essential components of any educational provision. The removal of school milk in the early 1970s was the harbinger of a retreat from traditional school services which has now extended to school meals services, instrumental music lessons and swimming activities, together with a major part of the once-extensive 'extra-curricular' programmes.

The significance of these services can be seen when looking at ways in which private and commercial educational organizations market themselves. They draw attention to sports facilities and swimming pools, library services and extra-curriculum activities. Where it is difficult for potential buyers to distinguish between the basic curriculum offered by rival private schools, these supplementary services are a prime means by which schools provide their 'unique selling proposition'.

Schools and colleges in the state education system should also look carefully at their support services when planning their marketing strategy. They need to recognize which services are needed and wanted by parents and students. They can then help to market a 'package' in which due attention is given to both core and supplementary services. Attention should also be given to the better presentation and delivery of these services. Low-cost improvements can include the 'branding' and 'styling' of tangible products, from stationery to sports gear. Many schools have returned to a distinctive school uniform in order to provide a clearly branded image for the school – and have involved their students in styling that image.

The final category of services provided by schools and colleges comprises those which make use of the institution's facilities in order to generate extra income or satisfy the needs of non-traditional customers. There is a strong tradition in English education, going back at least to Henry Morris' 'village colleges' in Cambridgeshire, of community schools and colleges. This ranges from the shared use of facilities to the more complete integration of educational, social and recreational services for a whole community. Recent legislative changes have made it possible for institutions to keep their earnings (previously taken back by some LEAs) when they have hired out their premises and other facilities. Activities undertaken specifically to raise additional income are examined in Chapter 9. At this point, attention is drawn to the need to take these services into account when planning the institution's overall provision. Not only are many schools and colleges heavily dependent upon the earnings from these services, they also benefit from the goodwill engendered as the community makes use of its local school or college.

Price *all this*

This second 'P' is the element of the 'marketing mix' most likely to present problems to educational managers. It comprises two distinct components: *costing* and *pricing*. The former involves the calculation of the real costs of providing a service, whereas the latter fixes the amounts to be paid by the consumer. These are very different activities, even for non-profit organizations such as schools and colleges. This section looks first at some general problems associated with costing and pricing in educational organizations and some basic principles, before going on to examine costing issues in detail, using a framework for examining each element of a costing system. It then goes on to consider pricing issues, looking first at the customer's perception of price before going on to explore the key elements of a pricing policy and the setting of pricing objectives.

The moneys brought into an institution by or on behalf of a student do not necessarily represent the sums expended in providing the service. Some students will have more spent on them than they bring in, others less. The introduction of formula-based financial delegation schemes and the increase in fee levels in higher education to levels which approximate more closely to the real costs of providing the service have sharpened institutional anxieties here. Concerns have focused upon the inequities of such crude assessments of 'per capita' costs. A marketing perspective should help the institution relate income and expenditure to organizational mission and customer needs. The key tasks are, on the costing side, to seek as close a match as possible between institutional spending and customer benefits and, on the price side, to ensure that customers are charged sums in line with the institution's objectives.

Problems and principles

Until very recently, most institutional managers had only very limited experience of and even less control over either costing or pricing. They are now having to learn to manage them where, under new schemes of financial delegation, their success is dependent on their ability on the one hand to attract and retain students, and on the other to do this with very limited and shrinking resources. Careful costing and pricing are essential skills in this situation.

The real costs of providing an educational service at institutional level have only recently been examined seriously. Local authorities had to attempt this in order to prepare their schemes of delegated finances as required by the Education Reform Act. The unfortunate officers commissioned to do this soon found that a significant part of the necessary information just wasn't available, and they had to make crude estimates – which, not surprisingly, attracted fierce attack from those institutions which consequently lost out in the application of the formula so derived. The problems had already been spelled out by Knight (1983), when he pointed out that:

> a school is a cost-accountant's nightmare: a labour-intensive, non-profit-making service organization, with ill-defined objectives, with uncosted and unquantifiable outputs and ill-costed inputs, in a strait-jacket of constraints and with an arthritic lack of flexibility in building and staff.

The statement is just as applicable to colleges, polytechnics and universities as it is to schools.

The efforts of the last 2–3 years have done more to engender more general appreciation of the scale of this problem than to resolve it. Financial delegation has transferred responsibility for most institutional costs to governing bodies and institutional managers, without necessarily providing the information base (particularly in terms of historic cost trends) from which sensible cost decisions can be made. Any organization whose purpose is defined in terms of service provision to customers needs to know what resources it has available to expend on these services. Formula funding approaches provide a global sum based upon the total number of customers, but unless managers know accurately just how resources are being consumed by the basic service delivery processes, they can do little to steer resources in directions of greater efficiency and effectiveness. Many institutions receive significantly fewer resources under schemes of local financial management, but do not have cost information available with which to identify where savings might be made and resources diverted.

In developing a strategy for costing and pricing, a basic need is information about costs at sub-institutional levels, which will not only provide data on the current costs of existing services, but will explain what happens to costs when new services are provided, or when the existing services are offered to more or fewer students – or to students with different backgrounds from those normally recruited.

In particular, institutional managers such as departmental heads need to know the real costs of providing their basic educational services – their courses. It is not just that information is difficult or impossible to obtain, although increasingly managers are now able to calculate the real costs of providing so many hours of tuition per student/pupil. They really need to know the effectiveness of this expenditure in terms of customer benefits. But there is as yet no established methodology for calculating this, and no signs that such a methodology would be acceptable even if developed. Should benefits be measured in terms of receiving the service, i.e. attending the course, and, if so, should the level of student attendance be an indicator of effectiveness? Or should output measures be used to determine effectiveness? In other words, is examination success or success in obtaining a job at the end of the course the most appropriate basis for calculating 'output costs' and customer satisfaction?

The dilemma is a real one for those with marketing responsibilities in a school or college. Vigorous recruitment policies might be successful in attracting lots of students, leading to large classes and low unit costs. If, however, this leads in turn to low satisfaction levels and high course drop-out and examination failure rates this is likely to be counter-productive. If, on the other hand, recruitment is restricted to those all-but-certain to achieve good end-of-course grades, this can mean high unit costs and possible failure to address that aspect of the institution's mission which promotes access to groups of customers normally excluded from that part of the education service.

Three distinct principles shaping a costing and pricing strategy for educational organizations are considered next. The first is that the institution's mission and the resultant policies should be actively promoted by this strategy. It is very easy, at a time of prolonged financial stringency in public sector education, to lose sight of the institution's educational purposes in the frantic search for more savings and ways of cutting costs. Decisions about possible cost reductions must always take into consideration their impact on the quality of the service provided to customers. Those with marketing responsibilities are well placed to contribute here only if they have the necessary cost information at their fingertips. Similarly, services should be priced to meet institutional objectives, so that price changes must take into account those objectives and not just short-term cash-flow crises.

The second principle is that costing and pricing decisions must take full account of the market and of current and forthcoming changes in that market. The basic objective is to attract as much business as the institution is capable of delivering effectively, at a price which at least covers the real delivery and development costs of the service – though the price may be paid only in part by the user and largely or entirely by taxpayers, sponsors and others. The fact that the market is an imperfect one, with most educational institutions unable to influence – except at the margins – the prices charged for their services, does not detract from this principle. Most education is still free at the point of delivery throughout the state-funded school sectors, in colleges for those under the age of 19, and for most undergraduate courses in higher education. The price for these services is usually fixed by central government agencies, and consumers commonly do not know what that price is. None the less, there are costs incurred by customers and their sponsors (parents and employers), and these need to be appreciated within the institution in shaping its marketing strategy.

A third principle underpinning any marketing strategy is that costing and pricing decisions should involve, wherever possible, those directly providing the service. When teachers and non-teaching staff appreciate what is being paid by customers or those paying on their behalf, and how much is being spent in return to deliver the service, they are much more likely to look for ways to achieve the twin goals of providing value for money and a high-quality service. Another important aspect of staff involvement is that surpluses, when generated, should be redistributed in ways which encourage and motivate the teaching and non-teaching staff whose efforts produced those surpluses.

All this implies that costing and pricing decisions should rest within the institution as far as possible. The introduction of financial delegation schemes for schools and colleges encourages this. Governing bodies now have much more control over pricing strategies under local management of school and college schemes. In practice, the broad policy for pricing should rest with the governing body, while the detailed strategy for delivering that policy should be the responsibility of the establishment's management.

This requires that those responsible for course management should be made aware of the real costs of their courses, and of the ways in which those costs are calculated. This should include development costs, and should then be examined in the light of the product life-cycle, the nature and costs of certification, the market penetration and the product differentiation.

It also requires that the basic financial controls are located within the organizational structure, where they can be influenced by those with marketing responsibilities and related to the other elements of the 'marketing mix'. It is important that the financial aspects of marketing form part of the responsibilities of the marketing managers and team, rather than being hived off to be the exclusive concern of the financial controller. The financial and marketing functions come together here. Concerns for efficiency – normally a prime consideration for the financial manager – must not be ignored. Nor should the concerns for effectiveness which should shape the decisions of the marketeers.

Costing

Marketing managers constantly face enquiries about costs. In a college of further education they need to know what it will cost to lay on a training course in interpersonal skills for security guards in response to a request from the guards' employer. A polytechnic course tutor needs to know the cost of equipment and staff training in order to upgrade a computer studies module. A primary head needs to know how much it will cost to reduce class sizes to below 30 pupils per class. A secondary school head of department needs to know whether a residential field course can be afforded. These are all decisions in which the likely customer benefits have to be weighed against the costs of providing them.

Costing is an accountancy exercise, which in no way inhibits the creativity needed to undertake it effectively. It is possible to organize and present the costs incurred in delivering a service in a variety of different ways in order to bring out different features of the service. This section explains some of these ways. It is important that the organization and presentation of costs should not rest exclusively with the accountant and finance director. Cost information can be arranged in a number of different ways. The implications of organizing finances in different ways need to be understood by those with marketing responsibilities, because only then can they ensure that customer interests are being taken into account and that institutional objectives and customer needs, as well as financial probity, are being pursued.

This section may seem critical of some of those with specialist responsibility for an institution's finances. It does seem to be the case that the delegation of financial responsibilities to institutions has led to so much concern to avoid 'overspending' that short-term palliatives are being adopted, whose longer-term implications are likely to be damaging to both the institution's prosperity and to customer interests. After all, it was noted a decade ago that the threat of swingeing penalties for local authority overspending led to such caution among financial controllers at local authority level that there was a significant underspend – so that the education service nationally was deprived of millions of pounds. Care must be taken to ensure that this does not happen now that responsibilities have shifted to the schools and colleges. It is also the case that the response to new responsibilities by many institutions has been to bring in a financial controller, bursar or management accountant from outside the education service. This means that financial decisions may well be made in ignorance of their educational consequences unless they are influenced by those who both appreciate customer needs and understand costing and pricing.

The distinctions between a number of different ways of designating costs need to be understood when preparing a marketing strategy. This section examines staffing costs first – the major costs incurred in almost all educational activities. It then goes on to examine the differences between *direct* and *indirect* costs; *fixed* and *variable* costs; *full* and *marginal* costs; and *opportunity* costs.

The determination of accurate *staffing costs* is usually the most important and commonly the most difficult task facing educational managers in this area. The identification of real staffing costs requires knowledge of the actual staff to be deployed, their salary grades, and the numbers of hours accounted for (which could differ substantially from the hours actually involved in the activity), or the actual payments made to them in respect of the work. To this must be added the 'on-costs' incurred by employers' national insurance and superannuation contributions, which currently amount to between 15 and 20 percent of salary. In most educational establishments, staffing costs are further complicated by the ability to substitute part-time staff for many activities, whose costing basis is quite different from that of full-time staff. Direct costs should also include preparatory and development costs for activities absorbing staff time, although these can be divided between several activities if the programme being developed is likely to occur regularly or at least to be repeated on one or more occasions.

Non-teaching staff costs involved in delivering the service also need to be calculated. These can include secretarial and administrative support, technicians and welfare assistants, etc., calculated again to include on-costs.

All these are *direct costs*: costs incurred directly in delivering the service. Other such costs will include:

- training materials, including handouts, course texts, video/film purchase or hire, computer materials and time, etc., and the use of special equipment, including computer and audio-visual and other technical equipment where this is hired or bought in especially for that course; and
- promotional costs related directly to a specific course or activity, including printing, advertising and the costs of specific promotional events.

Additional costs might include residential and transport costs needed for a service, e.g. a college weekend training course or a school residential field course.

Other costs are not so directly related to the course. There is no clear-cut distinction between these direct costs and *indirect* costs, but rather a gradation. The use of premises may be calculated as a direct cost only where special space requirements are required and have to be bought or hired. Otherwise, this is included as an indirect cost along with water, heating and lighting, cleaning and maintenance, and rents and debt charges. Catering and reception/switchboard costs are further indirect costs along this spectrum.

The costs of teacher in-service and initial training are normally difficult to attribute to specific activities, as are the institution's central administrative costs, including managerial and secretarial salaries, postage, telephone and stationery. The staff development costs (courses, conferences, attachments, etc.), including costs of staff release for such activities, have become increasingly significant parts of institutional budgets.

When trying to attribute costs to a specific activity, a fairly arbitrary line is drawn to separate direct from indirect costs. The obvious direct costs (and particularly the staffing costs which comprise at least two-thirds of overall educational costs) are calculated as accurately as possible. The remaining indirect costs or 'overheads' can then be worked out as a standard calculation of a percentage of direct costs. It is usually much easier to estimate an overhead cost as a percentage of direct costs, rather than to attempt to calculate separately the proportion of the institutional costs deployed in a particular activity.

A full calculation of indirect costs should also in theory include a proportion of central government and local authority costs in administering the education service. These constitute the administrative, advisory and inspectorial services along with specialist services such as those provided by the Careers Service and educational psychologists. They also include the initial provision of the premises and government-borne in-service and initial training costs. Local authorities have traditionally required some proportion of income generated by schools and colleges from lettings, full-cost courses and the like as a part payment towards these indirect costs. The delegation of financial responsibilities has made this requirement more problematic, although some authorities are attempting to continue to seek such recoupment in some areas.

Central government is now forcing LEAs to delegate a larger proportion of the total education bill to individual institutions, with the result that they are no longer able to hold back funds to pay for central services. This is causing a shift in local authority approaches, as they begin to look at these as services to be marketed to schools. This, in turn, is leading to the development of marketing strategies by the local authorities, in order to pay for their central services.

A distinction within the 'direct costs' category is that between *fixed costs*, which do not alter according to the numbers of participants, and the *variable costs*, which do. This distinction becomes important to marketing managers when calculating the cost of a service on a 'per capita' basis. The staffing costs are fixed costs, which do not usually change whether there are 20 or 30 pupils in a class. Variable costs only usually become important when they include residential accommodation, as when costing a field course, or when substantial materials and equipment need to be provided as part of the service, e.g. a computer or expensive textbook for every student. Otherwise, these are confined to the proportionally low costs of handouts and consumable materials.

However, this approach holds good only when considering specific services within institutions, such as a course. When the institution as a whole is considered, most costs become variable costs, as the numbers of teachers and non-teaching staff vary according to the numbers of students. Marketing planners must then identify the perspective from which institutional (as opposed to sub-institutional or departmental) objectives and customer needs might best be met. Cost definitions most in tune with that perspective can then be selected as a basis for planning this aspect of the 'marketing mix'.

A common controversy in institutions establishing a more entrepreneurial stance is whether *full costs* or *marginal costing* should be used. The distinction is seen most clearly when considering a new student joining a school. Is the real cost of that student calculated by taking the total costs of running the institution and dividing it by the new total number of students? Or should you calculate just the extra expenditure needed to meet the needs of that specific student – the textbooks and materials but not teaching costs because the student goes into classes already staffed, so incurring no extra staffing expenses? The former calculation gives a full cost figure: the latter a marginal cost figure.

In further and higher education, this leads to disputes where the providers of a new activity such as a short course want to cost it only on the basis of the additional direct costs incurred in providing that course. They argue that the other costs – central administration, premises, etc. – would be incurred whether or not the course takes place, so should be discounted. The course should, they argue, be costed on a marginal cost basis. Financial controllers, on the other hand, are likely to argue that the new activity should carry a full proportion of those indirect costs and should be costed on a full-cost basis. A marketing judgement is needed to resolve this. It may be legitimate in some cases to calculate marginal costs rather than full costs for certain forms of provision, particularly where, for example, a special course involves some attendance on an existing award-bearing programme, the costs of which are already accounted for. The attraction to providers of using a marginal costing is enhanced when the reduction of apparent costs leads to resultant 'surpluses', a proportion of which can then be used by the providers. However, no school or college can support for long the hidden subsidies that marginal costing incurs. A properly calculated full cost basis is the only long-term basis for calculating service provision. If a new activity needs to tempt customers by offering low prices (as is possible at the initial stage of the 'product life-cycle'), the costs of this should not be disguised by artificially low cost calculations.

Opportunity costs is another useful concept in examining the cost elements of a marketing strategy. They apply most commonly to the deployment of staff, particularly where market analysis indicates that new or upgraded services are sought. The opportunity costs of developing new activities include all those activities or developments that the members of staff are prevented from doing by spending expensive time on the proposed activity. They can be high, and need to be considered in relation to the conditions of service as well as salaries of the staff. If staff are to be deployed on activities which commonly do not mesh comfortably with the rather rigid constraints of the school/college calendar, it can present more than just timetabling problems. It can render valuable resources unavailable for other activities, whose value short-term or long-term might well be a lot greater than that of the activity on which they are deployed. For example, in post-school education, the opportunity costs of tying highly skilled staff to regular year-long weekly teaching commitments can be high in terms of the income they are thereby unable to generate through short courses and consultancy. This has been one of a number of factors which has encouraged institutions to move to modular course structures, which provide greater flexibility of staff utilization.

Pricing

Pricing is a policy-making task, not an accountancy exercise, and it requires a range of marketing skills. These include a clear understanding of the market and how it operates, and the effects of pricing decisions on customer perspectives of the service on offer. Pricing policy must be directly related to institutional mission and policies. It needs to take account of both financial and non-

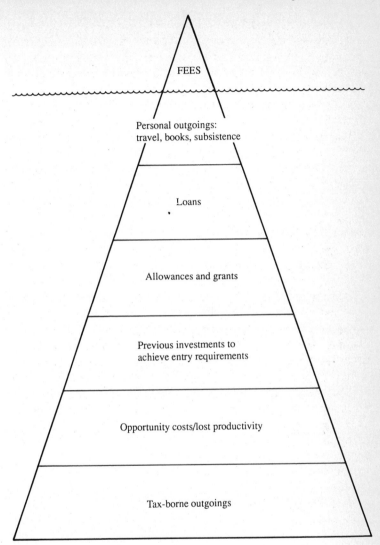

Fig. 8 The educational 'priceberg'.

financial benefits such as 'reputation', 'goodwill' and market dominance. More important than any of these, however, are the considerations in terms of customer benefits.

A starting point is to look at price from the customer's point of view. A 'priceberg', as indicated in Fig. 8, is a device for doing this. This indicates that the amounts of actual cash paid out for an educational service form only the small but visible tip of a far larger amount of costs to be perceived and considered by customers – or those parents and employers calculating on their behalf. In pointing to previous investments, it recognizes, as did Adam Smith two centuries ago, that the real price of everything is the toil and trouble involved in acquiring it. While at the base are those substantial outgoings paid for out of taxes.

The long-established British tradition that most education should be free at the point of delivery is gradually being eroded. Some school-based educational services such as instrumental lessons now have to be paid directly for by the consumer. Student grants have now been replaced after much controversy by a loan scheme to cover travel and subsistence costs, but the tuition costs of a higher education course for a UK or European Community student are still paid for by the taxpayer through central and local government, rather than directly by the consumers and their parents. Most full-time education from the ages of 5–19 in public sector schools and colleges is also charged to central and local government – and hence to taxpayers.

In consequence, consumers are only interested in the full price of education when they contemplate using the services of the private sector. Consumer decisions here are made more complex by the purchase decision being perceived as buying more than just education. Intangibles such as status, easier access to higher education and improved social contacts have been identified as at least as important as the education itself on offer (Walford, 1990). The promotion of private sector institutions tends to emphasize these intangibles and their relative scarcity, as is discussed in the next chapter.

For public sector schools and colleges, the main price considerations relate to the efforts needed to obtain entry qualifications for higher education, some parts of further education and selective secondary schools. In the schools sectors, travel costs and convenience are important, although their significance tends to decrease with the age of students. Travel costs are important, however, where local authorities refuse to pay travelling expenses for students wishing to attend an institution in a neighbouring local authority – another example of governmental intervention to impede a free market in education.

In post-compulsory education, time represents the major opportunity cost for consumers. A year spent having to repeat an 'A' level course or part of an undergraduate programme can mean lost income, as well as, in the latter case, the requirement to pay one's own tuition fees for the repeated year. There is little evidence of the impact of tuition fees on consumer decisions. A price-competitive market is most obvious in the areas of short course provision and postgraduate higher vocational education. In the latter, there is little evidence, for example, that higher tuition fees for MBA programmes deter employers, but rather that the fees reflect an informal perception of quality variations – prices seem to be set at the levels that the market will bear. In adult education, there is evidence that sharp increases in fees by local authorities coping with urgent financial crises have the effect of reducing demand significantly: a good example of short-term financial policies militating against agreed educational objectives.

Further complications occur when looking at the additional costs incurred by students and parents, when schools and colleges charge for service augmentation. A school uniform is one example of this, along with specified sports gear and the other items carefully listed as requirements placed on the parents of new pupils as they enter many primary and secondary schools. For some parents, substantial expenditure here might be a price barrier, and schools have developed strategies for helping parents reduce this expenditure, with discreet second-hand sales and bursaries. For other parents, such expenditure requirements can seem a surrogate quality measure: schools not requiring so many specified items may be perceived as inferior to those with lengthy and rigid specifications. Such additional costs were recognized when the government introduced a student loan scheme. The legislation included provision for a 'hardship fund' in both further and higher education, in order to reduce the price to those students and their families defined as qualifying for the fund's support.

The implications of the above are that, as has already been discussed in Chapter 3, the market for educational services is complex, and the considerations most likely to influence consumers are not necessarily those expected by educational providers. Price *per se* in the form of fees is only a major consideration in some of the remoter thickets of the educational jungle. Elsewhere, opportunity costs, travel costs including time, and the cost of supplementary services need to be taken account of when devising a marketing strategy. This process is examined next.

Any educational institution's policy needs to resolve two initial dilemmas or tensions. The first is whether the policy is to *maximize take-up* or to *emphasize selectivity*. In the former case, price barriers such as travel and school uniform costs need to be considered and strategies such as the 'hardship fund' referred to above need to be implemented to reduce or eradicate them. In the latter case, the institutional controls over student admission discussed earlier mean that it is only in the less savoury parts of private sector education that price operates as a major means for achieving selectivity.

However, price can be perceived as an indicator of quality. This is demonstrated by many institutions in the form of supplementary charged services, ranging from tuition charges for the non-statutory parts of the service such as instrumental and dancing lessons to uniform regulations. Government policies have reduced the impact of price in some ways in recent years. The Assisted Places Scheme made private education available to some students whose parents would otherwise have been unable to afford it. More recently, 'price rationing' for auxiliary services such as residential field courses, which restricted participation to those who could afford to pay, has been banned. The recent 'hardship funds' for further and higher education demonstrate further evidence of this policy.

As a result, the dilemma of maximizing access or selectivity is most obvious in those post-school sectors operating mainly on a full-cost basis, marketing non-award-bearing courses. For example, a college developing an income generation policy based on short training courses can choose between a 'stack 'em high and sell 'em cheap' policy where tiny surpluses per student are justifiable because of the very large volume of students passing through, or emphasize high-quality and consequent high prices to produce small numbers of clients, but substantial per capita surpluses.

The second tension is whether the policy is to *recover (most) costs* or to *maximize surpluses*. Partial cost recovery has been the most common basis for adult education fee structures, although there have been pressures to push these towards full cost recovery as mentioned earlier. More generally, pressure on resources in every sector has encouraged institutions to develop some activities which might generate surpluses, in the hope that they will compensate at least partly for the reductions in resources from central and local government.

A number of factors which deterred income generation and the quest for 'profit' have been eradicated or diminished. Until recently, many LEAs required that all or part of any surpluses generated by educational institutions were returned to the LEA as a part payment for the central services and institutional funding provided. This was, of course, a major deterrent to any quest for 'profit'. The government passed legislation in 1985 (the Further Education Act) to encourage further and higher education colleges to find ways around these constraints by means of the device of the 'college company'. It was hoped that this would enhance the flexibility of colleges with respect to both costing and pricing in areas where local authority policies inhibited enterprise. The impact and benefits of college companies are considered in Chapter 9.

The deregulation of educational financing through schemes of local financial management and the 'incorporation' of higher education institutions have freed schools, colleges and polytechnics from most of these local government constraints. At the same time, further reductions in government funding have made the need to generate additional income all the more important, to the extent that institutions from universities to primary schools are now far less dependent upon their local or central government funding than was the case a few years ago. Institutions now undertake some activities where no direct cost recovery is possible; other activities where partial cost recovery occurs; and still others where surpluses are actively sought, with prices set at levels that the market is estimated will bear. The appropriate balance of these activities demands sophisticated management, involving sensitive financial and educational judgements.

After resolving these two dilemmas, the pricing policy should be shaped by three major considerations: costs, the nature of competition, and known levels of demand.

Cost might be expected to be the most important influence on an educational pricing strategy. In fact, it is probably the least important for many institutions. The recent legislation in the UK has reinforced the price controls of both central and local government, the former through its higher education funding councils and the latter through government-approved formulae. The consequence of this governmental price fixing is that costs are tailored to match price rather than vice versa.

As a result, cost is of paramount importance in pricing only a limited range of educational activities. In these situations, 'break-even analysis' is the most common means by which prices are set.

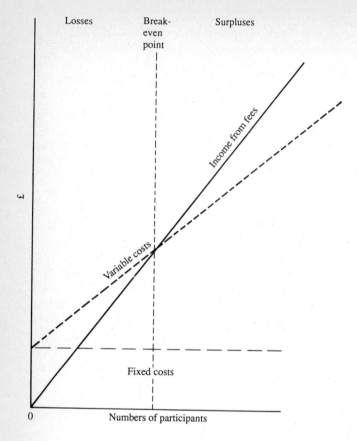

Fig. 9 Break-even analysis applied to conference planning.

This involves calculating, for example, the number of places on a training programme or at a conference which must be sold in order to cover costs at a given price level. This is done by establishing first the fixed costs, then the variable costs according to different estimates of the places to be taken up. A provisional price per place is then specified and the 'break-even' point at which income matches expenditure found. If this suggests that an unfeasibly high number of sales would be needed, the price can then be adjusted upwards. Conversely, if the provisional price would cover costs with relatively few sales, it either can be adjusted downwards or the providers can look forward to substantial surpluses! An example is provided in Fig. 9.

It is easier to calculate a price when the total number of participants is known in advance, as when preparing a short course for an employer. The total costs can be calculated, and a *mark-up* added to provide a surplus for the provider. All this requires, of course, as was stressed earlier, the ability to calculate fully and accurately all the costs likely to be incurred.

Prices should be set at less than the full costs only where there is a policy decision to provide the service. This might be in order to meet a high-priority institutional or LEA objective, in which case the nature and extent of the 'subsidy' should be clearly spelled out, or to offer the provision as a 'loss leader', e.g. to attract and prepare the institution for possible future larger and more realistically priced contracts. It is also possible to set a price at less than full cost where bridging funds are available to cover the gap between the price charged and the full costs. This can occur where the institution is very anxious to provide the service because of its value for staff development element. The staff development budget can then be deployed to account for any deficits. In recent years, a large number of government initiatives have provided partial funding, particularly in the areas of vocational training and consultancy for businesses. In these situations, colleges are becoming adept at helping employers obtain such 'topping-up' funding, and are able to offer the service at a price to the employer which is augmented by Employment Department or other governmental support. Indeed, an annual guide (*Paying for Training*) is published to indicate just what bridging funds are available and how they might be obtained.

The government's intention that education should be provided in a competitive market is making *competition* an increasingly important aspect of pricing policies. Although most prices are still fixed by central government regulations and local government formulae, the limited areas of price flexibility do enable consumers to consider price variations when shopping around for a school or college. An institution's 'intelligence service' needs to find out the prices being asked by the competition, and the quality of service being offered at that price. Pricing strategies can then be determined in terms of charging the 'going rate', attempting to undercut competition, or even to charge more than competitors where it is believed that consumers perceive high prices as an indicator of high quality.

The development of bidding or tendering systems in further and higher education adds a further pressure on the institution marketing function, to ensure that its information is more than adequate and its strategies are right for that particular market. Polytechnics and higher education colleges are now required by the Polytechnic Central Funding Council (PCFC) to bid competitively for additional students, with the price as the most important criterion. Competition in further and higher education for industrial training courses, consultancy and contract research is increasingly competitive. Educational institutions compete with private consultants and research and training companies, as well as between themselves for these contracts.

Strategies for reducing the real price asked of consumers are important ways of competing effectively, but it requires a good understanding of just what consumers perceive as that 'real price'. Some head teachers are able to compete effectively for pupils by promoting the school along the local bus routes or by persuading bus services to alter their routes to extend to a potential catchment area. In higher education, low-cost student housing seems to be an increasingly important incentive, and some institutions are benefiting by being able to offer this.

The level of *demand* will also influence the pricing strategy. The private education sector is well used to the most eligible institutions charging very high fees for tuition and subsistence, taking advantage of high levels of demand far in excess of their limited capacity for schools such as Eton, Harrow and Millfield. Higher education is moving slowly towards forms of demand-led pricing in areas such as management and business studies, where high levels of demand enable universities and polytechnics to 'enhance' fees over a standard rate, particularly for postgraduate courses and vocational courses paid for by employers. At least one institution (Anglia College of Higher Education) has been reported as levying an extra registration charge on all its 10 000 students.

It is important to be able to forecast likely levels of demand, and this is an important part of any marketing research strategy. Sudden unforeseen changes of demand can cause severe problems, as happened in further education a few years ago when demand for mechanical engineering courses dropped suddenly. Demand can be stimulated, of course, by new product development and effective promotion strategies, requiring investment by the institution to provide and spell out benefits. The more strongly the benefits are perceived and wanted, the higher the price that clients are likely to be willing to pay for those services.

An issue of some delicacy for institutions is whether to adopt a *differential pricing* strategy, whereby different clients are charged different prices either for broadly the same service or for different levels of service. This follows logically the maxim of charging what the market will bear, but it depends heavily upon the different client groups being strongly segmented – and unlikely to be in touch with each other. There are well-established differential pricing approaches in higher education, but these are based on the differential costs of, say, medical and history courses rather than being demand-led. Differential prices are used in the post-school sectors when marketing short courses and conferences. Interestingly, the normal strategy is for lower prices to be offered to early applicants, rather than the theatre and travel business approach of low prices at the last minute to sell the remaining places.

Pricing decisions are likely to take account of previous pricing decisions, costs, the prices charged by competitors (if known), estimates of likely demand, and the extent to which institutions and departments are allowed to retain any surpluses or 'profits' thus made for educational development and investment. It is important that those with marketing responsibilities and an understanding of customer behaviour are involved when setting fees and other prices: it is not a task for a finance officer alone. Indeed, it may not be a task for the finance officer at all. It is important that current government policies are understood when considering prices, but this is not enough on its own. Forecasts of future plans and policy intentions at central government level are important in a highly volatile environment, where the market is in part inhibited by governmental price fixing and at the same time providing more opportunities for imaginative pricing strategies. In post-school education, the new Training and Enterprise Councils are likely to have a growing influence on the provision of vocational education and training, and at the time of writing it is not clear whether they will encourage a freer market with more price competition or will follow government practices and use their considerable financial powers to fix prices.

An effective pricing policy will need a comprehensive and accurate *marketing information system*. This is important for all aspects of educational marketing, but becomes particularly crucial at the pricing stage. Accurate and full information needs to be accessible concerning costs, levels of demand, ways of stimulating those demands, and actual and potential competition. Most important of all, accurate information is needed internally, concerning the capabilities and availability of the key resources of the institution – the teaching staff in particular – in order to deliver quality services commensurate with the price being asked for those services. In turn, such information must contribute to the institution's evaluation system and to its staff development policies, so that those key resources can be enhanced and otherwise developed in order to meet the needs of the community served by the institution.

The pricing policy is a vehicle for staff motivation. It should be communicated to all staff who are likely to be involved in costing and pricing decisions and in the consequences of such decisions. It should be reviewed regularly in the light of marketing research information. Finally, the policy should be flexible, so that it is possible to experiment with pricing in manipulating the elements of the 'marketing mix'.

Place

This element of the marketing mix includes all those features of a school or college which influence the accessibility and availability of the service. It is concerned with the location of the institution and its appearance, as well as the facilities on offer. It is also concerned with those services offered outside the institution and the means by which they are distributed. Each of these aspects of the concept is considered in turn.

Premises and the environment of education

The distribution of educational establishments is very largely a reflection of past needs and former political decisions. It is almost impossible to shift the location of a school or college. Closure is usually the fate of institutions whose location has become inconvenient or inaccessible for its customers. The costs of abandoning an inappropriate location are now so high that it rarely happens. Its more frequent occurrence in the past is sometimes recorded in a name related to the original location, such as Westminster College, the Methodist college of higher education now located outside Oxford. Today, institutions are more likely to try to adjust their services to changed circumstances than to move to a new and distant site. However, institutions can extend their services by providing them on additional sites and in new locations, and the implications of this are considered later.

The appearance of the institution, in contrast to its location, offers abundant opportunities for improvement. Schools and colleges have realized in recent years that their appearance is an important influence on people's perceptions of the institution's quality. This has been reinforced by concern at the serious deterioration in the quality of the fabric of the UK's public sector education service. Regular local authority-funded repair and maintenance programmes have provided easy targets for financial cuts, and have, in consequence, largely disappeared. These short-term and short-sighted responses have been described as a national disgrace by many, including the government's own inspectors, in the annual reports from HMI. The 1988–89 Annual Report of HM Senior Chief Inspector of Schools points out:

> The state of secondary schools is a problem. HMI judged two-thirds of the schools inspected to have unsuitable accommodation and in just less than half of those the problems were serious and adversely affecting the quality of the work in one way or another. . . . Accommodation in FE varies markedly within and between colleges. Some teaching areas are well designed and modern while others are old, drab and in need of refurbishment. . . . In HE the state and suitability of accommodation are matters of serious concern. Two-thirds of the polytechnics have poor accommodation and more that is unfitted for its purpose. . . . Much of [the accommodation] used by the youth and community services is old, drab, badly maintained, and inappropriate for its purposes. (DES, 1990a)

The lack of maintenance is normally most obvious in the delapidated and unpainted external appearance of the institution, leading to immediate problems for those wanting visitors to receive positive first impressions of the place. Educational managers have worked hard and imaginatively to ameliorate these problems. Despite the financial cutbacks, more care and thought is shown in attending to the appearance of the internal physical space than was the case a decade ago.

Primary schools have demonstrated how much can be achieved with very limited resources but with a lot of energy and imagination. Children's artwork is displayed extensively throughout classrooms and public spaces, while teacher contributions have been the elegant preparation and mounting of such work, and the organization by which displays are regularly changed. Part of the inspiration behind this has been the encouragement and motivation of pupils by displaying their work. This in itself is a potent marketing device. Children and their parents are likely to be more satisfied if their work is displayed prominently and feel that their efforts are being rewarded. Visitors to the school not only walk into a cheerful and welcoming environment, but are able to make some instant judgements about the quality of the work being undertaken at the school.

Primary schools have also tended to develop an attractive *atmosphere* by paying attention to all the senses. Primarily this is part of the development of sensory and aesthetic appreciation among pupils. It is also, however, a significant marketing ploy, even though its significance as such may not be appreciated by all primary school teachers. The importance of creating an appropriate, welcoming indoor environment can be witnessed in those shopping malls carefully designed to encourage shoppers to linger and make use of a wide range of services. Piped music engages the ear, bakery shops project the smell of baking bread, fountains and expensive indoor trees improve the view and sculptures encourage the sense of touch – all in the interests of marketing.

With none of the heavy investment in costly resources seen in the shopping mall, primary schools are able to create equally distinctive environments. Peaceful music plays as youngsters move into the hall for morning assembly, wall-hangings and displays encourage children and visitors to touch and smell. As parents are increasingly exhorted to visit several schools before deciding which one to send their children to, the creation of such a friendly, welcoming atmosphere is just as important to the school as it is to the restaurant, hotel or shopping centre which spends heavily to create just such an atmosphere.

A further significant improvement in primary schools, and one more obviously related to improved marketing, has been the removal of those notices which deter visitors, and their replacement with welcoming signs and notices. Secondary schools and further and higher education colleges have also made progress in improving the appearance of their premises. These are larger than most primary schools, and need clear signposting not only for visitors but also for the students themselves in their initial weeks at the place. Institutions have invested in improvements in their foyers and reception areas, to make them more welcoming and to direct visitors more readily to reception facilities.

Further education colleges have given particular attention to the improved organization of their enrolment procedures at the start of the academic year. It can still happen that potential students are deterred by the lack of signposts to the college, a packed foyer with no directions as to where to attend for enrolment, and then long queues to sign on for the course of their choice – only to be told at the end of this that the course is full, the would-be student is insufficiently qualified, or that she has attended on the wrong day!

In general, institutions need to examine the following aspects of their premises when examining the 'place' and coming to decisions about the strategies needed to improve this element of the marketing mix – and to identify the resources necessary to do so:

- external signposts in nearby roads and transport terminals to the school or college;
- clear indications at several points on the institution's boundaries as to where the main entrance can be found;
- clear indications on entering as to where the reception area and receptionist can be located;
- clear internal signposts to the administrative area, departmental territories, staff room, toilets, refectory and any specialist rooms, particularly where these are for use by occasional visitors, such as a parents' room in a school or a careers advisory service;
- waiting space in a well-tended foyer or reception area for visitors, with seating, information about the institution and arresting visual displays, whether of student art, collections of sports trophies or staff publications; and
- clear labelling on internal doors, indicating uses as well as numbers.

A basic principle is that intangible educational services should be made more tangible by associating them as specifically as possible with a distinctive space. Many schools and colleges recognize this when they provide identifiable space for student groups. Once again, primary schools are most experienced in this, because of their organization into classes which stay together on one base for a year.

This is not only organizationally convenient, it also recognizes a very basic human need for territory. It is not just the class group which is important to its members, it is the tribal territory represented by the classroom which the group occupies for a year or more. Ardrey (1966) drew attention to the 'territorial imperative' as a basic drive which people share with other animals, and suggested that much human behaviour is motivated by the need to possess and maintain territorial rights. Handy (1986) translated this notion of 'territoriality' into organizational terms, pointing out ways in which people tried to satisfy their territorial needs by both physical manifestations – office size, carpets and trappings – and in psychological terms. The latter might include the possession of information and of the 'territory' visible only on an organizational chart.

Much organizational politics can be explained in terms of battles to expand organizational territories. Once such territories have been gained they are staked out with tangible symbols of the new owner. This is most marked when a company is taken over by another, and the winner's corporate image replaces that of the loser.

Staff and students in educational organizations demonstrate this need. Staff rooms can contain the inviolate territories of particular teachers, marked by a favourite chair or desk. Staff groups might convert a store room into a refuge for one department in the school. Students seek social spaces in which they might gather between classes, and mark out the space if possible with their posters and graffiti. In seeking to ensure customer satisfaction, education managers recognize the strength of these territorial needs, and do what they can to provide and furnish appropriate spaces for both staff and students.

Taking this further, institutions can try to 'brand' the service so that a distinctive space is supported by artefacts which reinforce a 'corporate image'. This is now a standard feature of hotel and restaurant chains, airlines and department stores which carefully (and at great expense) pay specialist agencies to design the image from logo and promotional literature to staff uniforms and carrier bags. This is considered in more detail in the next chapter. It can be seen in educational organizations most clearly in some of the better private and public sector conference and management training centres, which provide a comprehensive service similar to that offered by a good hotel.

All this costs money, and resources on this scale are not available to most public sector educational institutions. The examples of primary schools referred to earlier suggest, however, that teachers are unusually skilful at making a lot from a little. Some attention to the territorial needs of students pays dividends in obtaining commitment, and to identifying with the place at which education is delivered as a tangible manifestation of the service received. This has long been recognized by those teachers and institutions which have campaigned successfully against vandalism and graffiti, by enhancing the quality of the buildings and increasing the commitment of both staff and students to the institution.

One further aspect of an institution's environment needs to be noted: the influence either of geographical location or specialist facilities which make a location so distinctive that the establishment is sought out by customers despite its relative inaccessibility. The most obvious example of this is the specialist field studies centre. Its location next to or within an area of special scientific or geographical interest draws customers who need to make a first-hand study of the scientific or geographical phenomena to hand. A well-established string of such establishments offer specialist laboratory provision as well as residential facilities, in locations such as the Yorkshire Dales, Pembrokeshire Coast and Lake District.

A rather different form of specialization occurs where specialist facilities are provided which are sufficiently unusual to attract students nationally and even internationally. Agricultural colleges, art schools, ballet schools and specialist engineering and catering departments in colleges of further and higher education combine expensive facilities along with the specialist staff able to make use of them for educative purposes. Some private schools similarly make much of the lavish laboratories, computer suites, sports facilities and swimming pools in attempting to attract customers.

Distribution channels

The concept of 'place' in the traditional marketing mix is used in a rather different sense from the ways in which it has been considered so far. It refers to 'placing' goods where they can be obtained by purchasers. In other words, it is concerned with the *distribution channels* which transfer goods from manufacturer to consumer. Soap powder, cars and chocolate bars all need to be distributed to sales points by efficient marketing channels. Marketing decisions are needed about both the nature and location of the sales points from which their goods will be distributed and the transport systems which convey their goods to those sales points.

There is no equivalent tangible movement of goods in the provision of educational services, but there is still a need to consider
whether the service is available in the most appropriate places,
conveyed along the most effective routes, to its users. The notion
of 'distributing' an intangible service such as education is complex
and ambiguous. From one perspective, the nation's schools might
be looked upon as 'sales points' from which pupils receive a
National Curriculum manufactured by the government, in much
the same way as a Ford dealer distributes, repairs and services the
products sent there from the central manufacturing plants at
Dagenham and Halewood. That is not the perspective pursued
here. Rather, educational institutions are examined as places
where educational provision is planned, albeit using standard components shaped elsewhere (the National Curriculum, etc.) and in
part delivered – but recognizing that the educational processes do
not take place entirely within the establishment, and need not be
undertaken there at all in certain circumstances. This section looks
from a marketing perspective at ways in which education is distributed to its markets. It also examines ways in which it might be
distributed in order to provide more accessible and convenient
services for its customers.

Although it is difficult to shift the physical location of a school or
college, there are two significant ways in which services might be
distributed to match more closely the needs of customers. The first
is by establishing 'satellite' or 'outreach' services in premises
where particular groups of customers can obtain the service more
conveniently than at the main site. Adult education has long experience in this approach, taking its evening classes out to its customers in village halls, rooms above pubs, primary schools and
shopping centres. The principle of taking education to the people
is also well-established in some parts of further and higher education. The notion of 'work-based learning' is gaining currency, but
has long formed part of some colleges' vocational training, where
the college has provided training on an employer's premises using
the employer's equipment and working in partnership with the
employer's staff. Higher education pioneered forms of certificated
non-vocational education, through 'extra-mural' and 'university
extension' programmes. More recently, the polytechnics have expanded since their establishment 20 years ago, by acquiring premises over a wide area in order to deliver their services to as broad
a group of customers as possible.

Another way in which education might be distributed more effectively is by extending the period of time when it is made available. Schools and colleges have been criticized for the long periods when their premises are closed and their services unavailable. The 190 days' schooling of the English pupil is compared unfavourably with the 245 days attended by a Japanese pupil. Some schools have experimented with 'continental day', starting earlier and leaving the afternoon free for extra-curricular activities, but these experiments have not been popular with working parents and most have been abandoned. Flexibility over the year, with possible four-term approaches have been discussed, but are restricted by the timing of national examinations.

In post-school education, constraints are fewer, and further education in particular has extended its working year, with many colleges now open for 48 or 50 weeks per year. Changes in staff conditions of service have provided the flexibility to enable courses to be staffed over this period. This, in turn, means that courses need not always start in September, but, where an employer wants a training course starting in April and continuing through the summer until November, this can be provided. These changes are further examples of the increased responsiveness of colleges to their customers' needs, and this extends to different daily and weekly work patterns, to meet the needs, for example, of shift workers. Courses can, therefore, start early in the morning or run at weekends.

It does not follow, however, that all customers must come to the establishment, wherever it might be located, in order to use the services. Only a very small number of children are educated exclusively at home, usually by their parents, under arrangements which require government approval. The private tutor who traditionally resided at the homes of the rich and educated their children is now almost an extinct species. Some forms of home-based tuition continue to thrive, including instrumental music tuition. The main forms of home-based learning are now, however, those provided through 'distance learning' or 'open learning' where the correspondence text and electronic media provide the tuition.

The Open University offers what is probably the best known example of an education service distributed to the homes of its students. Its headquarters at Milton Keynes has no students, only staff involved in the preparation and maintenance of its distance learning programmes. It uses the media of radio, television, correspondence texts and audio- and video-cassettes to convey learning to over 100 000 students, who are supported by a network of tutors and counsellors. The approach has been much imitated throughout the world. National 'open universities' have been established in many countries based upon the UK model. More recently, the model has been used to provide vocational education and training at below degree level through the government-established 'Open Tech' and Open College, while the polytechnics have come to-gether to establish a distance learning 'Open Poly'. Organizations providing these national learning networks can operate either through direct contact with their customers, as does the Open University for most of its activities, or can use intermediaries. The 'Open Tech' is heavily dependent on its networks of further educa-tion colleges for delivering its services.

As well as the establishment of these national open learning networks, individual institutions have tried to reach their cus-tomers – or to reach out to new markets – by developing their own open learning programmes. Over the past decade, it has become increasingly common for further education colleges to provide some courses by 'open learning' approaches. These include both the provision of nationally available packages, distributed through further education colleges, as well as the provision of home-grown packages, developed by college staff. These initiatives have been stimulated by support from organizations such as the Training Agency, which attempted to promote learning approaches leading to qualifications for those groups who find it difficult to attend a college – shift-workers, the home-bound and those living or work-ing in isolated communities far away from any college (Hebridean Islands, oil-rigs and overseas work placements).

A rather different approach to the distribution of educational services follows a commercial services model of selling by *franchis-ing* and joint ventures. Higher education institutions are coming to arrangements with other organizations, normally further educa-tion colleges but occasionally private training organizations, to deliver a course planned and validated by the university or poly-technic. The college buying the franchise pays a proportion of the student fees to the parent institution in return for the use of the course and usually some monitoring and external examination. Thus a small private South London college specializing in training overseas students franchises a Diploma in Management Studies from a London polytechnic. Kingston and Leicester polytechnics are among the growing number of higher education institutions which have franchised courses to further education colleges – commonly the first year of a degree programme, or perhaps the first 2 years of a Higher National Diploma (HND) course. Franchise arrangements are also used to deliver educational services overseas, especially in countries where the governmment places restrictions upon the movement of citizens to study abroad. This involves a local college or university delivering a programme developed and specified by, for example, a UK or US university. The joint venture is a variant on this; for example, East London Polytechnic delivers a part-time MBA programme to Singaporean managers in Singapore, in partnership with a local management institute.

In both types of arrangement, teaching is undertaken by using staff approved for the purpose by the franchiser or senior partner. This is likely to include both local staff (from the further education college or overseas institution) and staff from the 'source' institution, and the qualification at the end of the course is exactly the same as if the course had been undertaken in that institution.

7 | Promotion and public relations

Chapter 6 described ways in which schools and colleges might develop attractive programmes of study and other services, price them appropriately and ensure their availability in convenient formats and in welcoming and accessible locations. All this is of no avail if potential customers do not know what is on offer to them. This chapter focuses on ways in which institutions might communicate effectively with their customers and those who act on their behalf. The chapter starts with the customer, looking at the processes involved in deciding whether or not to use an educational service. It goes on to examine some key aspects of the communication process, and its relationship to the decision-making processes by which customers become committed to educational programmes. The range of strategies by which educational institutions can inform and persuade their potential customers is explored. An examination of a range of specific promotional techniques follows, including advertising, personal selling and the uses of publicity materials. Their integration and organization in the form of a promotional plan are considered next. Finally, the related issues of public relations and media relations are examined.

The education service is not renowned for the effectiveness of its communications with the public. Its problems stem in part from the fact that most adults have spent at least a decade of their lives in educational establishments, and not surprisingly believe that they know a great deal about them – even (or especially) when this experience occurred half a century ago.

Some educationalists have responded defensively to this by trying to establish a mystique of 'professionalism'. They argue that the organization and delivery of learning is complex and can only be understood by those who have received special training, and then been inducted into the professional secrets. This is supported by the use of jargon and mysterious acronyms, understood only by fellow professionals. The successful mystification of the legal and medical professions, in order to restrict entry and boost income, has long been gazed at enviously as a target to which to aspire by educationalists holding to this perspective.

The lessons of the past decade are that this approach has been singularly unsuccessful. Education is much more tightly regulated than a decade ago. Teachers in every sector are paid less in relative terms, and their conditions of service have worsened. Industrial action to counter these trends failed dismally, resulting only in the loss of support of the public at large.

A marketing perspective rejects the mystique of a professionalism which resists clear communication with, and involvement of, customers and clients. The need for, and some steps towards, a more effective process of communication with the public is discussed later, in the section on public relations. Before that, the processes by which customers decide whether or not to take up an educational service are examined, along with ways in which educational organizations might help to shape customer decisions.

Customer decision making

Customer choice is an important consideration in every sector of the education service, now that local authorities are no longer able to restrict choice by insisting on school 'catchment areas', and students and their parents are encouraged to shop around for the best school or course. Some understanding of the decision-making processes, whereby potential customers decide to register for an educational course or attend a particular school or college, is necessary if educational marketeers are to inform and persuade their potential customers.

A great deal of effort and resources have been invested in order to understand how customers make decisions. As might be expected, most of this has been by commercial organizations, trying to find ways of persuading customers to buy their products. A number of models of customer decision making have, in consequence, been developed (e.g. Engel *et al.*, 1986), but their applicability in the context of educational decisions has not been tested. It is more difficult to generalize about these, partly because of the range of decisions involved in an educational career, from the decision about which nursery or infant school to attend through to decisions about adult education classes and postgraduate research projects.

If educational institutions are to help with these decisions, by providing appropriate information to those involved in making the decisions, they need to understand something about the processes involved. This requires knowledge of the people involved in making a decision, the steps involved in coming to that decision, the kinds of information sought and used at each stage, and the communication channels by which that information might reach the decision makers. Each of these elements is considered in turn.

Educational decisions are both important and complex. Who knows the extent to which youngsters at the ages of 4 or 11 are able to influence their parents' decision about which infant or secondary school they should attend? At least at these stages the option of not being educated at all is not available – and very few parents and pupils select the option of education at home. From the age of 16, there are more options open to potential students, and more influences on those deciding whether or not to stay on at school, go to a further education college, seek work or anticipate unemployment and a training scheme. This presents real problems for those wanting to influence such decisions. Promotional efforts to inform parents of the benefits of colleges of further education are of little avail if the key decisions are made by the students and their friends, or their teachers and career advisers in the secondary school.

This is why a detailed understanding of the market by those preparing promotional strategies is so important. The approaches which may be effective for recruiting secondary pupils may have little impact when used to recruit 18-year-olds to a university. Techniques which attract 16-year-olds in South London may fail dismally when used in rural Somerset. The decision-making processes need to be understood in order that appropriate messages are conveyed to those making the decisions.

The issue for educational marketeers is that there are usually several people involved in the decision to attend an educational

establishment or register for a course. Distinctions between consumers and customers were drawn in Chapter 1. Effective promotion requires that these distinctions are clearly understood. Those
involved in making the decisions about which school to attend or
course to take may well be different from the end-users. The key
people involved at each stage of the decision-making process need
to be recognized and the influences on those decisions understood.
Effective persuasion requires knowledge of those likely to be involved at different stages, and then the ability to prepare messages
appropriate to each group.

It helps to look at the processes involved in coming to a decision
from the decision maker's point of view. Several elements are involved in deciding which course to take or which school to attend.
Customers and their advisers first need information about the options open to them, when seeking to satisfy a range of needs and
wants that are unlikely to have been precisely specified. The information should help them to clarify these needs and wants, at least
into different categories of priority, and also to establish the criteria
by which the options might be evaluated. The identification of *needs*,
prioritized in terms of importance, *choices* (the options open to
them), *criteria* for evaluating the options and *actions* needed in
order to obtain the preferred option, all contribute to the decision
making. An 11-year-old and her parents, in trying to decide which
secondary school to attend, will commonly have at least three or
four options from which to choose. An 18-year-old seeking a degree
course could well have dozens from which to select.

Information is needed in making these choice decisions, about a
host of issues ranging from transport convenience and uniform
requirements to perceived quality of teaching, levels of discipline
and likelihood of congenial or familiar classmates. To these must
be added the longer-term needs to which the 'right' choice of
school or course will provide access – such as the next educational
stage, career prospects, social contacts and future social status. In
all of these areas, parental needs and criteria for making comparisons are likely to differ substantially from those perceived by
their children – whether they be aged 11 or 18. And at each age
friends, relations, teachers and other advisers will probably offer
differing advice according to their personal experiences, prejudices
and priorities.

Those marketing the schools or courses under consideration will
need to know a great deal, if they are to assist with the decision

making. The needs expressed by prospective students, their parents and friends, the priorities given to those needs, the criteria by which the choices will be judged and the other options under consideration, all need to be known if an effective promotional strategy is to be designed. The information needs to be collected, sorted, organized and analysed using sound research strategies, in order to ensure that those seeking help get the information they need at the right time, and in the appropriate sequence.

Customers and their parents, employers and friends may all offer conflicting advice. There are also specialist advisers whose perceptions need to be appreciated by marketeers. The influence of careers advisers has been identified as particularly significant as 15-year-olds decide whether or not to stay on at school or go to college or to work. Friends and peer-group pressures help shape choices of school and college, and choices of options within the institution. The media influence decisions when they pillory a school or publicize a controversy, drawing attention to criteria that the other decision makers might not otherwise have considered.

Educational institutions also influence choice decisions. Education is a service over which the providers still retain a remarkable number of controls as to who might make use of it. Many parts of the service remain free at the point of delivery – but that does not mean that they are accessible to all who might want to obtain that qualification or attend that school. The education market is manipulated by providers to restrict and direct consumer choice, leaving the key decisions, at least in areas where demand exceeds supply, in the hands of the head teacher or admissions tutor.

Institutions make decisions about who to admit to their courses by establishing admissions policies and entry qualifications. In practice, these are adjusted in response to demand, so that a popular course at a popular polytechnic may attract many more applicants than there are places – and the total number of places available is limited by staffing resources, polytechnic policies or government regulations. Promotional strategies in these circumstances may be to emphasize the stringent admission requirements, whether they be the fee requirements of expensive private schools, the 'A' level passes required by a university department or the demonstration of 'aptitude' sought by some city technology colleges. The purpose of promotion here is to maintain the high reputation of a service based upon its exclusivity, and to advertise its availability to sufficient potential customers to retain control of admission in the hands of the providers. The aim is to create what economists call a 'relative good', whose value is achieved not so much by its intrinsic value as by its scarcity – like American cigarettes or jeans in those countries where their import is restricted.

The decision-making process is made more complicated by the fact that it is difficult to describe *one* simple (or even complex) process at all. Traditional theories about how decisions are made describe 'rational' approaches comprising a series of recognizable decision-making stages. This posits that needs are first of all articulated, and then are prioritized. Information is collected about ways of meeting these needs, and is analysed using pre-selected criteria or weightings, in order to evaluate the options according to the extent to which they meet the most important needs. A provisional choice or preferred option is then evaluated, possibly by testing it with other people to ascertain their attitudes. This assists the identification of possible or potential problems and the likelihood of their occurrence – in other words, against the risks involved. All these are taken into account when making the final decision and commitment.

This presumes a rational process through which decision makers progress step by step. But real life is not like that. Some people do go through the stages identified in textbooks advocating 'rational decision making' (e.g. Kepner and Tregoe, 1986). Most of us recognize that much of our decision making is governed by impulse and intuition, and that the thoroughness of the decision-making activity is not necessarily related to the importance of the decision. We might compare canned soups by carefully studying their volume, price and chemical additives before deciding on the brand to buy. However, our choice of house (or partner) is not shaped by any such rational appraisal. For some, educational decisions might be so routinized as to require no analysis at all. One youngster will expect unquestioningly to attend the same school and follow the same courses as her elder sister, while her next door neighbour visits five or six schools, has long discussions with teachers and parents, and then a lengthy period of consultation with friends and family, before deciding on the same school.

Those with responsibility for marketing educational services do not, therefore, have models readily available to enable them to plan the ways in which to influence customer decision making. They need to develop methods of communicating with all those involved in ways which take account of the variety and complexity of the processes involved. They need to recognize that the decision to seek a service not automatically available involves the potential customer in *risk taking*. The promotional messages must appreciate that this element of risk will lead to risk avoidance behaviour – so the messages need to include forms of reassurance. Suburban parents may need to be reassured about the security of their offspring, should they travel some distance to an inner-urban college, while at the same time the youngsters may need reassurance that they will not be treated like school-children at the college.

Communicating with customers and clients

In trying to make sense of these complexities, use can be made of some of the simplistic devices used to help salespeople operate effectively. A starting point is a basic marketing model, summarized by the acronym 'AIDA'. This draws attention to four distinct processes in the communication processes needed to obtain a sale. They are:

- first the need to get *attention* (A);
- then to hold *interest* (I);
- then to arouse *desire* (D); and,
- finally, to obtain *action* (A) – the sale.

It is unlikely that any single communication medium or message is so powerful that it will take a customer from initial awareness through to commitment to buy. Hence the diverse and sophisticated techniques used to sell not only expensive goods, over which customers might be expected to ponder carefully before buying, such as cars, but also low-cost, mass-produced products such as soap powder. This is not to argue that education needs to be sold like soap powder, only that the communication processes are similar in bringing services to the attention of potential users, and that different methods are likely to be needed at each stage.

This simple model can then be considered along with the various methods for conveying information available for marketing. Four basic approaches can be identified: *personal selling*, *advertising*, *publicity* and *promotional events*. They are likely to vary in their impact, according to the stage reached in the communication process. Advertising might be a valuable way of attracting the attention of a lot of potential customers to an adult education programme. It is less likely to involve people to the extent that

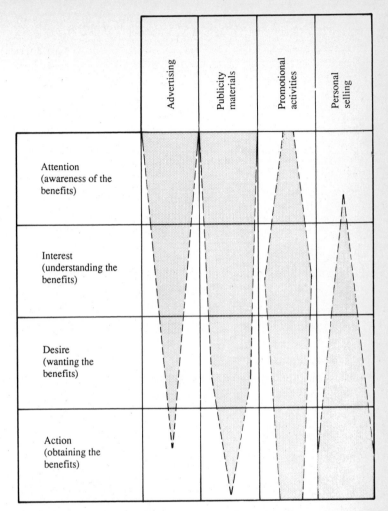

Fig. 10   The promotion process.

they will commit themselves to a year of evening classes without further persuasion. At these later stages, a promotional event such as an open evening, with personal selling – discussing the course with someone involved in providing it – is likely to be more effective. The relationship between the stages of communication and the available methods is summarized in Fig. 10.

Figure 10 also provides a framework for examining the relative importance of the promotional methods at each phase in what is

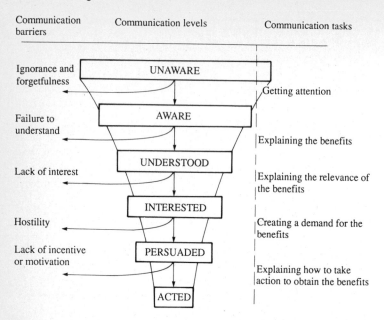

Fig. 11 Communication stages (adapted from McDonald, 1989).

normally an annual marketing cycle. The initial efforts to draw attention to the next year's courses usually take place some months before the start of the academic year. Interest-raising activities then follow, in order to shift people from awareness of the opportunities available to interest in taking part. The desire to enrol for a particular course, or in a particular school or college, may need to be shaped by rather different strategies. The processes by which the student signs up for a course or school commonly require different arrangements again. Furthermore, the nature of customer resistance differs at each stage, as Fig. 11 indicates. An analysis of the methods deployed at each stage can be used to determine ways in which the promotional strategy might be improved. This should lead in turn to the preparation of a promotional plan, as is explained below.

An important element in designing appropriate communication methods is that the target group decreases and becomes more precisely defined at each stage in the communication process. At the initial awareness stage, a very large group of people may need to be contacted, even where market segments have been carefully selected, although only a small proportion of these will show interest, and only some of these will go further and desire the service. Even fewer will eventually take action and use the service.

Methods which reach large numbers of people as efficiently as possible are likely to be employed at the initial stage, while the shift from desire to action may need one-to-one persuasion. The first stage in marketing an educational service may need no more than to let people know that a service or institution exists. Advertisements may be used by groups of schools which do no more than list their existence and location, and by further education colleges listing the courses available. Door-to-door delivery of leaflets can make householders aware of adult education services in their neighbourhood. Publicity materials might be stacked in libraries, post offices, supermarkets and banks.

Once people have become aware of a service's existence, they need to be told of the benefits and opportunities available to them. This will attract the interest of a more specific group than those aimed at in the first stage. For example, an advertisement may make large numbers of people aware of an FE college's courses for 16 to 19-year-olds, but only those in or approaching that age band, and with children or employees in the age group, are likely to be interested, and of that group only a proportion will go beyond this to want to use the service. These are the people who will go through the decision-making processes discussed above. Having been made aware that their needs can be met – after first having been helped to recognize that they have those needs – the promotional strategies must then provide the information required by prospective customers and their advisers in order to make those decisions.

Promotional strategies and techniques

All this points to the need for a range of promotional strategies. Marketing is a creative process and the educational marketeer's creativity can be taxed to the utmost when trying to inform such a variety of customers and their advisers with such limited resources. In the next section, each group of techniques is examined in turn, and suggestions made about situations where they might be employed – but this needs to be prefaced by the warning that there are no obvious prescriptions about the strategies and techniques to use at each stage of the communication process. It is necessary that these strategies and techniques are co-ordinated and that a promotional campaign is *planned*. Some suggestions for the organization of the promotional plan are made later.

The basic promotional techniques can be categorized, as in Fig. 10, into four groups. *Advertising* involves the purchase of space or time in order to convey messages to potential customers. *Publicity materials* are distinguished from advertisements in that they are targeted and distributed more precisely to potential customers. *Promotional activities* include all those events organized mainly or specifically to promote the organization and its services. They frequently provide an opportunity for *personal selling*, where face-to-face contact with prospective customers allows an individualized approach to promotion. The first two approaches are impersonal and allow only one-way communication, so that it is difficult to identify even where they have reached, let alone their impact. They need, therefore, to be complemented by the latter two approaches, which allow for two-way communication and can be more precisely targeted and evaluated. Each approach is considered in turn.

Advertising

Advertising costs money. Most educational institutions advertise, but more usually to recruit staff rather than students. And for most schools, even that advertising is handled by the local authority, although under schemes of financial delegation schools and colleges now have greater freedom to place their own advertisements, the price of which is having to pay out of their own budgets for them. These advertisements need to be recognized as part of the institution's promotional strategy. They need, therefore, to present a distinctive and consistent image, with careful thought given to their design. Institutions which spend large amounts on advertising can obtain professional advice by using an advertising agency to place all institutional advertisements for staff and students. There are no extra costs, because the agency gets its income from commission paid by the media, and it is likely that the agency can negotiate better advertising rates than can the institution directly. An agency will also advise on the advertising budget, in return for handling all advertising – but few agencies are likely to be interested in the modest advertising budgets of most schools.

Advertising for students is a relatively recent phenomenon. Higher education institutions agreed to ban advertising for first degree courses throughout much of the 1980s, but increasing competition for students has led to the agreement being ignored, and to increased expenditure on advertising by most polytechnics, colleges and universities. The main advertising vehicles available to schools and colleges are the press, television, radio, the cinema and spaces on buildings, buses, parking meters, etc. Each medium carries a price tag. Precise calculations need to be made when trying to decide whether the expenditure would be worthwhile and which medium to use. These calculations need to be incorporated within the promotional planning process, as discussed below.

Advertising is likely to be more effective in gaining awareness than in achieving action, but action might result directly from a successful advertising campaign. The promotional plan should provide a framework in which the objectives of an advertising campaign are specified and target market segments identified. The next task is to identify the advertising medium likely to reach those target groups most effectively. The advertising media need to be identified, costed and evaluated according to their capacity to penetrate market groups. Most organizations selling advertising space or time provide detailed information about their audiences, broken down in classic market research practice by age and sex. Furthermore, the advertising industry provides a series of standard guides, notably *BRAD* (British Rate and Data), which contains both audited circulation figures and full details of advertising costs in the media.

The decision as to which medium to use will be determined by matching market penetration against price, and by assessing the capacity of the medium to convey the desired message to the target groups. An institution's budget is likely to restrict the options open to a school or college. Television and the national press are relatively expensive advertising media, which reach such extensive audiences that the target group forms only a tiny proportion of the total audience. Only national advertising campaigns, such as the government-funded drive to attract new teachers (with the televised message that 'teaching brings out the best in people') can bear the cost of this approach. Local radio and local newspapers offer the advantages of being less expensive than television and the national press, and of matching more closely the target groups sought by most educational organizations. Cinema has advantages for post-school organizations, in that its prime audiences match those target groups commonly sought by further and higher education establishments.

The medium very largely determines the message. The message conveyed in a 20-second local radio advertisement is quite different from the slogan carried on the side of a bus. This is another reason why it is so important to establish precise objectives at the outset. If the objectives point to a fairly specific message, this will restrict the choice of media. If, on the other hand, the message is no more than that the institution exists, a parking meter may offer appropriate space – as long as the message is targeted at drivers. The intangibility of education as a service makes it crucial that the messages are clear, simple and unambiguous. The temptation to pack as much information and as many messages as possible into an advertisement must be resisted at all costs.

Nor should the messages involve lots of words. Education is understandably prone to over-emphasize the importance of words at the expense of pictures and symbols. The visual images used in commercial advertising, and particularly in cinema and television advertising, provide powerful examples of effective word-free messages. Where the advertisement's purpose is to draw attention to benefits, these need to be the benefits sought by potential customers – so the messages need to be shaped by the institution's marketing research.

The timing of an advertising campaign is crucially important. Most advertisements are ephemeral. A radio slot lasts no more than a few seconds, and even bill-boards are rented for no more than a few weeks. Local newspapers and specialist journals are read over a longer period than national papers, which are usually disposed of within hours of being bought. So, once again, marketing research is needed in order to discover the period when the target groups are most likely to be receptive to the messages conveyed. This relates both to the time of year and the time of day. Radio and television have strong daily listening and viewing rhythms, and these are demonstrated in the 'rate-cards' provided by those selling advertising time.

Finally, advertising has a role to play not only in reaching out to prospective customers and their advisers, but also in influencing employees and current customers. The impact of advertisements on these groups must be taken into account when preparing any promotional material. If the advertisements are effective, they will trigger interest leading to enquiries – and those enquiries are more likely to go directly to the institution's students, teaching and non-teaching staff rather than to those involved in designing the advertising campaign. For this reason, the messages carried by advertisements must not only be understood by employees and students. They must also reflect their views if the promotional efforts are to be supported. The quality of any education service depends upon the skills and attitudes of those providing the service, and they need to be reassured that their work is appreciated. Similarly, students who have already signed up for the service need reassurance that they have made the right decision. Advertisements can help to provide that reassurance. At the very least, they should not cast doubts in the minds of those already within the institution. It would be unfortunate if a message stating that a college's courses will be much improved next year led students and staff to feel that they were receiving and providing an inferior service at present.

Publicity materials

Publicity is a form of promotion which is part of the broader area of public relations. Some aspects are dealt with under that heading in a later section. The preparation of publicity materials by schools and colleges is now well established as a cyclical activity. All schools are required to produce annual brochures and handbooks. Further and higher education institutions invest heavily in the publication of attractive prospectuses, supported by a vast array of brochures, leaflets and course directories in every conceivable format. One estimate suggests that higher education alone spends at least £5 million per year on its annual prospectuses.

Annual reports are becoming established as vehicles for promoting higher and further education institutions: so much so that an annual award is offered by the *Times Higher Educational Supplement* and KPMG Peat Marwick McLintock for the best annual report. Schools make rather similar use of their newsletters to parents and even of their school magazines.

The preparation of effective educational publicity materials requires, most importantly, honesty. A couple of years ago, West Sussex trading standards officers reported that eight private schools made a total of 15 bogus claims about their academic achievements and sports facilities. Dishonest claims may or may not be picked up by independent watchdogs. They will lead to dissatisfied customers and a poor reputation in consequence, when the realities of the educational experience fail to live up to the hype. Effective publicity materials spell out the educational vision and mission of the organization, with the further benefit that existing staff and students can be helped to recognize that vision more clearly and then promote it.

In designing effective materials, it is necessary to identify precisely the services being promoted, the target audiences, the images to be projected (and the reasons why) and the vehicles by which materials will be distributed. In selecting the messages to be projected, care should be taken to ensure that:

- text is used sparingly, written clearly and is jargon-free;
- the use of space and headings is planned carefully, with expert graphic design help – the costs of such are slight in relation to the impact gained from good presentation;
- graphics are used selectively (professionals are likely to underestimate how difficult it is for others to make sense of organizational charts and route maps through modular programmes);
- sketches and photographs are prepared with care, by creative talents;
- the 'unique selling proposition' is spelled out clearly; and
- the institution's identity is emphasized with the use of a distinctive 'logo' or other repeated device for underlining its distinctiveness.

Many institutions now recognize the impact that video images have on their respective customers, and commission the preparation of 'promotional videos', to be used at promotional events. The investment in these has been considerable, with major higher education institutions targeting different videos at different market segments, e.g. the videos aimed at East Asian students emphasizing study facilities and career opportunities, while the versions for UK students draw attention to the social life and recreational facilities!

Other organizations put together at lower cost audio-visual (tape-slide) presentations, for use at promotional events and on visits to feeder schools. Educational establishments are usually rich in many of the talents needed here: the clear diction and presentation skills of many teachers can combine with the design and artwork skills of art departments, and the photographic talents often found in the staffroom, to produce attractive and professionally produced in-house promotional materials. The acquisition of desk-top publishing facilities by increasing numbers of schools and colleges provides further opportunities for developing, at relatively low cost, high-quality publicity materials – as long as it is recognized that technology is not a substitute for creative talent.

Publicity materials incorporate a host of ways in which the institution's image and messages can be conveyed to customers. Institutions only rarely have the opportunity to design or change their 'brand name'. A number of polytechnics took the opportunity to do this when they were removed from local authority ownership in 1989. Most institutions, however, from primary schools to universities, now use a corporate 'logo'. This needs to be clear, striking and simple – a combination of virtues not easily achieved, and testing creative talents to the full. Increasingly, the logo is accompanied by a short 'unique selling proposition' or 'USP', a pithy slogan, stating what makes the institution distinctive. Logos and USPs are only useful if constantly emphasized. They should feature on every letter or leaflet going out of the place, as well as all the publicity materials. The USP might be pithy enough to join the logo on every envelope going through the institution's franking machines, and might be included on handout materials and stationery provided for students as a part of their course.

Direct mail is a useful way of reaching carefully targeted market segments. Schools have traditionally used their own pupils as unpaid postal workers, delivering despatches to their own homes – and, on occasions, to neighbours. Publicity materials can be distributed in this way to prospective customers with the cooperation of feeder schools. Colleges also show ingenuity in using a wide range of methods for getting publicity materials into the homes of possible customers. These include making arrangements with newsagents for delivery with daily newspapers, using the Post Office's bulk distribution services, and buying mailing lists from the commercial organizations which specialize in preparing and marketing specialist mailing lists and databases, although these are expensive at up to £100 per 1000 names, and might not be up to date. Hill (1990) lists possible sources. It is now cost-effective for most institutions to establish and maintain computerized institutional mailing lists, now that even quite small schools have computers in order to manage their delegated finances.

Another useful strategy for drawing the attention of large numbers of people to an educational service is by obtaining the agreement of local supermarkets, banks, libraries, etc., to display leaflets and other publicity materials – often along with an attractive presentation of artwork by the institution's students, which brightens up the environment and draws attention to the providing school or college.

Promotional activities

A wide range of activities are grouped together under this heading. They are distinguished from advertising by the fact that they are designed to invite an active response from participants. They include the familiar 'open days' or 'open evenings' by which schools and colleges invite potential customers to come into the institution and sample their offerings. Some institutions have long experience of opening their doors in this way, but the impact is sometimes reduced by unclear objectives. An 'open' event which is designed to persuade potential students and their parents of the qualities of the school should be different from one which reassures existing parents that their children are making sound progress in a stimulating environment – and different again from the event intended to present a welcoming face to the community at large. When institutions, for all sorts of good reasons, try to combine all three messages into one event, congestion and some confusion as to its purpose are likely to result.

Conventions, *exhibitions* and *trade fairs* have become popular means for promoting post-school education. Commercial organizations now organize such events in the UK and overseas. Indeed, the worlds of education and tourism come close together with the development of 'package tours' designed, for example, for representatives of higher education institutions to promote their institution's attractions in three East Asian countries in 3 weeks. There are distinctive skills needed in making effective use of such forms of promotion, and these are indicated below.

Travelling exhibitions visit schools and colleges to recruit students for further and higher education. Increasingly, these are being adopted by secondary schools, whose roadshows now tour their 'feeder' primary schools, extolling the virtues of their particular brand of secondary education. A variant on this approach is the inclusion of the roadshow in a mobile bus or caravan, and the 'education shop' established in shopping centres and wherever else the target groups gather together. The 'education shop' is used by further and higher education and by local education authorities to provide advice and counselling. Adults are attracted into conveniently located premises, and helped to identify the forms of provision best suited to their needs, and the places where that service might most conveniently be obtained, in terms both of geographical location and mode of attendance. Financial advice might also be available, including possible sources of sponsorship. It is important that the objectives of an exhibition stand, mobile display or education shop are clearly and thoroughly analysed and specified before designing display materials and preparing stands. As with other forms of publicity, simple, unambiguous objectives should result in clearly understood messages.

Promotional activities such as those indicated above demand distinctive approaches and some particular skills, both in preparing the exhibition or event and in attracting passers-by to an exhibition stand. Sophisticated skills are required to present an institution in ways which persuade those showing interest to take the next steps needed to make use of the service (or persuade others to do so). These skills can be taught. They include the organization of the exhibition stand and the effective use of displays; the analysis of potential visitors and their needs; and the skills required to persuade passers-by to stop, look and listen – and then to ask questions which lead to their involvement in and desire for the service. The organizational skills necessary to log enquiries and respond promptly to them are further important requirements, while most important of all is the ability to persuade colleagues to give up their time willingly at evenings and weekends to staff promotional events.

Institutions need to ensure that those representing them – especially when that involves paying for an expensive senior manager to travel half-way around the world – have developed and can demonstrate these skills. This last point needs particularly sensitive handling, when one or more of the institution's senior managers believe that they are best equipped to attend the convention in Bangkok. Even a university pro-vice-chancellor might need some training in the skills needed there.

Personal selling

Promotional events provide opportunities for personal selling. This form of promotion involves face-to-face communication between salesperson and potential customer(s). The skills referred to above are particularly apposite when dealing with individual enquiries and when persuading a potential customer of the benefits to be obtained from taking up the service on offer. In one sense, it requires no more than the basic teaching skills required to convey information and ideas to one or more people, and to deal with queries when these ideas are not initially fully understood. On the other hand, this version of the art of persuasion might not come readily to some teachers (and non-teaching staff) whose styles are more effective as performers with a whole class as audience than in one-to-one encounters.

Central to effective selling is the ability to put oneself in the position of the 'buyer'. This involves finding out their perceptions, fears and needs through effective questioning. Only when these are understood can the advantages and opportunities of the educational service be presented as solutions to problems – in terms of benefits.

Objections can then be countered, and reassurances offered where appropriate. Reference was made earlier to the risks that customers take when making decisions. Personal selling is a particularly potent means for reducing these risks, and so easing the shift from interest to desire, and from desire to action. The fears and perceived problems of prospective students and their parents or employers can occasionally be so general in nature that they can be tackled through publicity materials or advertisements. However, they are usually personal, and may be due to misinformation (planted perhaps by a competitor). Only when face to face with these concerns can they be allayed and corrected. Those involved in personal selling may well benefit from training in the relevant techniques.

Personal selling is not just a task for specialist marketing staff. Indeed, such specialist staff may be less effective than those involved directly in delivering and in receiving the services, i.e. the institution's staff and students. There is some evidence that word of mouth is a particularly effective communications medium in service industries, and there is a general belief (though untested by research) that this is especially potent in promoting some educational services. The image of individual primary and secondary schools is heavily influenced by the views expressed by pupils and their parents. It is all the more important, then, that staff and students are encouraged to recognize their contributions to this aspect of an institution's promotion. This can occasionally be undertaken formally, with current students meeting with and guiding prospective students on visits and open days, or with staff and students on an exhibition stand or at a careers convention. But it can occur more pervasively when the staff and students, asked 'what is it like at X school?', are aware that their comments form part of the institution's marketing activities. Strategies for ensuring that all staff contribute effectively to their institution's marketing by conveying appropriate messages are explored in the next chapter.

Planning promotion

The organization of appropriate and effective promotional strategies requires careful planning. Within the broader context of the institutional marketing plan, some specific planning for the institution's investment in promotional activities is necessary. This requires, first of all, clarification about why promotion is needed at all. The widespread but mistaken assumption that marketing is only about promotion can only too readily lead to further assumptions that all marketing strategies must spend money on advertising and other kinds of publicity.

Rather different but frequently found problems arise from uncoordinated approaches, in which different people in different parts of an institution take promotional decisions. Without coordination and some planning, messages can easily be contradictory, as when one sixth form college head of department emphasized, when talking to prospective students, that the institution was highly selective and required good GCSE grades for entry, while at the same time a colleague in another room was telling students that entry qualifications were not important.

A basic requirement, as with any kind of planning, is the specification of clear objectives. These will be derived from the institution's aims or mission, and will refer to the steps needed to put into practice the intentions exposed in those broader objectives. The promotional plan should indicate, therefore, exactly how the institution intends to go about informing, persuading and assisting potential customers to take up the services agreed in other parts of the planning process. For a school or college, these are likely to make reference to ways of:

- reminding people that the institution exists;
- distinguishing the institution from institutions offering similar services;
- drawing attention to the benefits available;
- reinforcing or changing the institution's image;

- explaining the steps needed to take up the service; and
- reassuring those who have already taken up the service that they made the right decision, and should persuade others to do the same.

Once the objectives are identified and prioritized, it is then possible to plan a promotional strategy to achieve those objectives. This might involve a specific promotional campaign focused on a particular course, department or market segment. The organization of such a campaign requires, first, that the campaign's targets are clearly identified. This involves the identification of the target groups, and the reasons for contacting such groups. Is it to raise awareness, by letting them know that a college exists? Or is it to shift perceptions of an already well-known institution in an attempt to change its image? The provision of information is not a strong enough reason for investing in promotion – there have to be good reasons for selecting and disseminating that particular information, and this needs to be related to the institution's marketing goals.

Nor is the decision as to which groups to target an easy one. Even if the marketing research has enabled clear market segmentation, the complexity of the decision-making processes discussed above mean that one group of customers will be influenced by a variety of advisers, who are unlikely to be reached by the same promotional strategy or advertising medium as the principal target group. Careful planning is needed in order to plot the target groups against the messages to be conveyed, and then to calculate what kinds of activities are most likely to reach target groups at each communication stage, within the institution's staffing and budget limitations. The planning process requires investment decisions. In making these, the question should be 'what returns can we expect at different levels of investment?', rather than 'what can we get for a predetermined budget limit?'

A 'promotional mix' of activities will form the basis for the promotional activities. The framework offered in Fig. 10 suggests one way of going about this. The relationship between advertising, promotional events, publicity materials and personal selling needs to be worked out in terms both of a series of stages in the campaign and the relative costs of alternative approaches at each stage. The additional costs of training and staff time must be added to the more obvious ('above the line') costs of printing, advertising or exhibition stands. Personal selling is an expensive strategy, whose costs can too easily remain hidden 'below the line'.

The promotional plan needs to be properly managed. It needs to bring together all those promotional activities which, even in quite small establishments, are often undertaken without reference to each other. The person preparing the advertisement and job details/information pack as part of the staff recruitment process should do this with reference to the publicity materials being developed by those with responsibility for recruiting students. These in turn need to be related to and co-ordinated with the efforts of individual departments, course teams or admissions tutors, who might be developing their own promotional materials, leaflets and personal selling strategies. Without discouraging individual marketing initiatives, these must be co-ordinated to ensure that contradictory messages are not being sent to the same prospective students or their careers advisers. They are also likely to need technical advice to ensure that the quality of their output is up to the standard set by the institution. This is likely to involve the marketing staff in all sorts of sensitive political issues relating to course team and departmental autonomy. As is stressed throughout this book, political skills are an essential component in the educational marketeer's toolkit.

Finally, the plan needs to be monitored and evaluated. Regular monitoring is needed to identify the effects of specific elements of the strategy, while a full evaluation is needed in order to determine the next year's plan. The monitoring and evaluation strategies need to be planned at the outset, so that devices are built into promotional materials to enable their impact to be tracked. This can range from the receptionist responding to a telephone enquiry by asking for and logging the source of the information stimulating the enquiry, to questionnaires for incoming students in order to find out how they first heard of the course. It can include coding systems on return slips, short questionnaires to prospective students and their parents at career conventions, along with more extensive marketing research, not only on those students who were persuaded to sign up for a course, but on those prospective customers whom the promotional campaign failed to attract.

Public relations

Public relations or 'PR' is defined by the Institute of Public Relations as 'the planned and sustained effort to establish and maintain goodwill and mutual understanding between an organization and its publics'. It stands somewhat apart from other marketing activities, in that the 'publics' with which it is designed to relate extend beyond the groups of customers, potential customers and staff considered so far. The purpose of a PR function in any organization is to provide information about the organization to all who might be interested. Much of this effort is expended through the media, so that an important element of PR is *media relations* – such an important element that the two are often confused. The concept of PR, however, extends beyond the media to include:

- the preparation of informational materials and reports;
- the cultivation and lobbying of key decision makers;
- support for worthy events and organizations, such as charities; and
- 'issues management': the development of coherent viewpoints on controversial issues, to be communicated internally and externally.

Central to the notion of effective PR is the *image* of the organization. Effective PR is only possible if the image to be projected is clearly identified and specified from the start. It will be shaped in part by the institution's mission statement and stated aims. These need to be set alongside evidence from marketing research about public perceptions of the institution, where there is less than a perfect match between institutional purposes and public perceptions of those purposes. This provides a focus for PR objectives, as derived and refined from the institution's marketing objectives.

In developing a PR strategy, it is important to know why the public image is not completely in tune with the institution's view of itself. At times this might be very obvious. When student unrest at an institution has featured daily in the national media for weeks it is no surprise when recruitment collapses. At other times, rumours and whispering campaigns arise without any obvious cause, and careful research is needed to track down not just the initiators of such rumours, but the reasons why they were started and why they found receptive ears. Fortunately, even the most maligned institution can usually generate enough goodwill to make use of an intelligence network of staff, students and parents who can assist in the necessary detective work.

The establishment of the image to be conveyed through PR needs to be followed by the identification of appropriate vehicles to carry and project the image. The media are important here, but before examining media relations, other aspects of a school' or college's public relations are considered. These include the provision of written materials, the organization of PR activities, and the external demonstration of an organization's worth through the work of its staff and students.

Public relations techniques include the preparation and distribution of written material such as newsletters, annual reports and informational handbooks. Tilling (1988) draws attention to ways in which schools can build up PR libraries, with photographs and text on hand to support a continuous rather than spasmodic PR function. The resultant materials are barely distinguishable from more specifically promotional material in some organizations. Indeed, attempts to cut costs can mean that the two functions are combined in the one publication – usually with the consequence that neither function is achieved satisfactorily.

The use of such materials has to be judged with care. Many alumni have been deterred from contributing to their 'Alma Mater's' latest appeal for funds by the high quality and obvious expense bestowed on the newsletter, annual report and presentation pack sent with the appeal. On the other hand, too obviously impoverished an approach may convince would-be donors that the place is beyond all hope and incapable of making good use of any funds sent to it.

The image can be reinforced by goods available through institutional sales points. Items of clothing, stationery and souvenirs may be sold partly to raise funds (as discussed in Chapter 9) but also in order to project the institutional image, perhaps by means of a logo and short message across a sweat-shirt.

An important feature of effective public relations is the firm and clear stand taken by the institution on controversial issues – its 'image management'. Events which project the institution's image rather than 'selling' it to prospective customers include the charity events undertaken by most schools, from sponsored swims and silences to charity concerts and door-to-door waste paper collections. All these carry with them images of the school or college as an organization making an effort to support worthy causes, such as the disadvantaged, the local community or the environment. The selection of particular charities demonstrates the institution's current concerns and values. It might be necessary to overcome the school's natural modesty and to spell that message out rather more prominently. The ability to hide lights under bushels is not of much help to a marketing strategy.

Other organizations might choose to project a rather more 'academic' image, by supporting a series of lectures, conferences or symposia, whose purpose in part is to spell out the institution's significance in the academic community. Similar events include the annual prize-giving favoured by many schools and the degree ceremonies of higher education institutions. The significance of these is in the messages they project not just to the staff and students within the institution and the parents and friends invited along, but to the community at large. They can become grand semi-public platforms from which the institution can demonstrate its links with the great and the good, invited along to give away the prizes, shake hands with the graduates and receive honorary degrees. The location of the stage is an important element in shaping the institution's image, as North East Polytechnic demonstrated when it moved its degree ceremony from West Ham to the Barbican.

Another familiar form of PR is the appearance of senior figures from the institution – commonly the head teacher, principal or director – on national platforms. These might be as keynote speakers at well-publicized conferences or as members of governmental or other public committees, commissions, task forces and the like. The clear and repeated association of successful author, broadcaster, sports personality or even local politician with the name of the school or college at which they work goes some way to recompense the employer for the time lost in those extra-institutional duties.

Media relations

Contact with the media is not only a major part of any PR strategy; it is that part which most concerns educational managers. Many still hold to the view that any contact with the media is dangerous, and do their best to stay as far as possible from media attention. There is no shortage of evidence that unwelcome media attention can do a great deal of damage. It is also likely that an institution which goes out of its way to avoid such attention will arouse suspicion that there is something to hide.

As with other elements of marketing, media relations need to be planned, and these plans need to be integrated with other parts of marketing planning. Plans should include a developmental component, in which skills needed for effective media relations are enhanced. These include the visual and vocal skills needed for effective television and radio interviews, and the skills needed by press officers in order to prepare written materials and cultivate telephone contacts. Tilling (1988) makes some suggestions as to how a school press officer might be deployed and how media contacts might be scheduled. Keen and Greenall (1987) have similar advice for higher education. Stories carried by the news media can benefit an institution, because they are more likely to be believed than is advertising and other publicity material. It is necessary, therefore, first to identify the media likeliest to reach an institution's 'public', and then to examine the kinds of news stories carried there. A media relations strategy will then tailor news stories to the editorial policy of the local newspaper or radio station – these are the media that most educational institutions are most likely to deal with regularly.

The next step is to scour the institution regularly for stories which are likely to interest the selected media. Staff and student support is needed here. Such support is also necessary to manage the misplaced attempts at media publicity of some staff. A clear institutional policy is needed concerning staff contacts with the media. Otherwise the good intentions of an enthusiastic colleague can jeopardize all the institution's efforts, by sending out messages which contradict or cast doubt upon those projected by the media relations policy. And something more sophisticated than a simple ban on staff contacts with the media is needed if staff support is to be sought: the media relations policy must go some way to harness and make use of the quest for media coverage by some staff.

There are four ways of communicating with the media: by telephone, by face-to-face contact with journalists, by writing to the editor and by a press release. The latter requires careful preparation. It should be written with a clear and concise message, giving simple details of an event or activity and an attention-grabbing short heading. The news should be structured so as to make the main point in the first short sentence, followed by less important details – the sub-editor will cut the story from the bottom upwards. The story should answer simple questions (who, what, when, where, why and how). It should be typed double-spaced, on official headed paper identifying the source, with the release time and date indicated (state 'immediate' if that is the case). Before sending it off to the news editor, it must be double-checked for accuracy, clarity and brevity. And remember that newspapers love to know the age of those about whom they write! If a news release is accompanied by a photograph this should be a 7 × 5 inch black-

and-white unglazed print – or invite the paper to send its own photographer.

Good relations with the media depend upon some understanding of their priorities and deadlines. There is little point in delivering a good story to a weekly newspaper only hours after it has been printed: the story will have to wait over a week to reach the public, by which time it will probably be stale. Local newspapers sometimes have difficulty in filling their pages, and a head teacher or college information officer who can be relied upon for an extra item to fill those remaining columns can be a godsend to the editor – although do not expect this to be reciprocated by spiking a story harmful to the college. Newspapers are commercial organizations, and a good story sells papers, however much harm it might do to the school and its staff and students. A friendly editor who receives regular stories from a school is, however, more likely (though by no means certain) to check with the public relations officer a story whose inaccuracies might harm the school.

A word of warning should be sounded, in support of those managers reluctant to use the media. Most public relations staff in education are amateurs, except in the larger polytechnics and universities. PR is a responsibility tagged on to a string of other responsibilities, even where it is the province of a full-time marketing officer. Staff can be taken unaware and out-gunned on the rare occasions that their institution comes into the attention of the national media. In particular, the tabloid press operate in a highly commercial, excessively competitive environment unrestrained (at the time of writing) by regulation. The standards found in the local media cannot be expected. Skilful journalists will extract comments from unwitting staff and students and misinterpret events and actions. In these circumstances, head teachers, press officers and others contacted need to be prepared. If caught unprepared they should not hesitate to seek a few minutes' breathing (and planning) space, by promising to 'phone back when properly informed. Key information can then be collected swiftly, 'no comment' responses avoided, and clear unambiguous statements made – and upheld. The preparation of a formal press handout can sometimes help in these situations. 'Off the record' discussions do not mean that they will not be reported, and interviewees should not allow words to be put into their mouths by interviewers who are likely to quote them out of context.

Any institution unfortunate enough to be harried in this way is likely to need external help. Fortunately, this is usually available from PR professionals in the major professional associations and, for some LEA institutions, in their local authority's press office. Assistance in the preparation of a press release, and even the organization of a press conference, can be invaluable in these circumstances. An effective marketing plan will include contingency elements indicating ways in which schools and colleges might cope with situations requiring external support, and involve some contact with such resources before they need to be called on in an emergency.

8 | Involving staff and students

The previous chapters have focused upon the marketing of educational services to customers – potential students and their sponsors. This is the familiar image of marketing, involving the presentation of services to people outside the organization, who are then persuaded to buy the goods or take up the service. 'Internal marketing', the marketing of the institution's services to those already using them, and to those whose task it is to deliver the services, has been referred to throughout the book. It is the central theme of this chapter, in which the benefits of and strategies for involving first students, then staff are examined.

Its starting point is the examination of reasons for, and advantages of, involving both staff and students in the marketing affairs of a school or college. The nature of possible involvement is discussed, in terms which relate some basic and longstanding educational principles to a customer-oriented marketing perspective. Specific strategies for involving students and other users of institutional services are then analysed. The involvement of teaching and non-teaching staff is then explored, along with the staff development strategies necessary to ensure that the involvement of all staff in the marketing of their workplace is effective.

Why involve students in marketing?

One of the most distinctive features of education as a service is its heavy dependence upon the active involvement of its customers in the educational process. The government might require that all young people from the ages of 5–16 must attend school, but over 2000 days of compulsory attendance will have little impact unless the youngster is actively involved in the learning processes. None of the other major public services require the active complicity of their customers in the ways that the education service does. Learning involves a partnership between teacher and learner in which the learner, not the teacher, controls what will and what will not be learned. Contrast this with the relationship between doctor and patient, lawyer and client, or bank manager and borrower.

A further highly distinctive feature of the education service is its organization into groups of customers, brought together for long periods of time for service delivery, whose interaction with each other is at least as important to the student as the interaction with the teachers. The nearest equivalent is the travel industry's package tour, but this lasts a fortnight, while a class group might stay together for 5 or 6 years. Staff and students come together to form a learning *community*, and this gives rights and places responsibilities on all those therein. Educational philosophers have long studied the implications of this for the organization of teaching and learning. Some have drawn attention to the significance of this community in a democratic society as a preparation for democratic citizenship. These are not the arguments being proposed here. The perspective here is one which gives prime consideration to the interests and needs of the customers, not as passive beneficiaries of the education process but as active partners in managing their learning.

It is now almost universally understood that education is not a one-way process of transmission from teacher or textbook to student. Not only do students need to be actively engaged in a complex interactive process, the organization of modern learning at every level gives prominence to the importance of students as *providers* of that learning. The more extreme manifestations of 'learning through experience' have led to its having had a bad press, but both teachers and educational theorists recognize how important it is to encourage learners to build upon and apply their experience, whether it is a 4-year-old measuring water in a nursery class or top executives building a bridge together on an out-of-doors activity-based management training course, designed to enhance their leadership skills.

Furthermore, the social and interactive nature of education is exploited by all good teachers, who encourage their students to teach each other. Lively and busy classrooms in every sector of the education service are characterized by groups of students working together to solve a problem and by individual students helping colleagues to overcome a learning difficulty, whether it be a complex chemistry experiment in a university laboratory or the beginnings of reading in an infant class.

This aspect of customer as service provider goes further: primary schools have been very successful in bringing in the talents of outsiders to support the learning. A modern primary classroom is likely to include parents who may be teaching youngsters to cook, play chess or listening to them read. Grandparents provide graphic first-hand accounts of local history, while the local fireman and policewoman make their distinctive contributions to the pupils' learning. In short, education is a highly collaborative process, which may be organized by the teacher but which is provided by a large cast of contributors, including all the customers.

As customers are both users and providers of the service, they will have informed opinions on the quality of that service, and offer a valuable source of evidence as to ways in which the service might be improved and drawn to the attention of other potential customers. The Responsive College Programme (Theodossin, 1989) developed some simple instruments whereby these student perspectives might be sampled and analysed.

Some aspects of recent research into patterns of consumer behaviour might help to understand better student perspectives on educational provision. It seems that consumers of services start with a general and often very vague set of ideas of the attributes of a good service. These are then refined through experience of the service and through the suggestions of service providers. Eventually, the consumer acquires a clear model of what is wanted, and then applies that model against competing services on offer. The attributes can be related to the marketing mix, with reliability and consistency as examples of 'product' attributes, and atmosphere and accessibility as 'place' attributes.

Applied to the education service, this concurs with empirical evidence of student needs, and argues for the importance, first, of shaping pupil perceptions in the impressionable days when they first join a school or college, and then ensuring consistency and reliability of service. The welcome offered to university students in their first 'freshers' week, and the efforts made in the infant school to acclimatize new entrants, is in sharp contrast to the disorienting experiences faced by some 11-year-olds when they first enter some secondary schools. Students at every age need to be made to feel an important part of the educational community, and this needs to be structured so as to shape as quickly as possible their models of a quality service. Central to those models must be the active participation of the students in their own learning and the learning of their peers. Because students make such a contribution to the learning process, they will impart to others that model of good service. It has long been recognized that students are a school's or college's best ambassadors: it is up to the school to organize the messages to be conveyed by these ambassadors to the next generation of students and their parents.

Why involve staff in marketing?

The importance of staff in all service organizations has been discussed in Chapter 3, where it was summarized as the principle that the job must be sold to employees before they can sell to customers. Employees are thereby encouraged to adopt a philosophy that the service should be delivered as though the provider were at the receiving end. This philosophy is particularly important in services such as education, where virtually all the staff come into regular daily contact with the students. In these industries, the service is, in effect, the people who deliver it. However, many teachers and non-teaching staff in educational organizations do not necessarily recognize this; indeed, may not accept that they are indeed providing a 'service', associating the notion with 'serving', and even being 'servile' and a 'servant'.

A marketing perspective needs, therefore, to encompass the notion of *internal marketing*, by which marketing strategies are used to 'sell the job to employees'. As with the involvement of students, this is unlikely to occur effectively unless it is properly planned. Such planning involves an examination of the recruitment and selection procedures, for it is much easier to recruit staff with this philosophy than to develop it later. However, the provision of training and other forms of staff development also needs to be planned, including the development and enhancement of specific marketing skills and techniques. The purpose is to create a climate in which staff recognize that they all have marketing and service delivery responsibilities, and to indicate ways in which these responsibilities might more effectively be fulfilled.

Internal marketing is important in educational organizations where a plurality of values is represented, and where there has been dispute about ways in which education might be provided. At the simplest level, this means that students should not be drawn into those ideological and tactical disputes which occur at times in most educational establishments. It means that teachers need to recognize that, however important their professional concerns to deal with every aspect of a syllabus might be, they may have to curtail some elements where the students do not have time to learn everything – and this attitude of careful selection becomes all the more important now that curriculum planning must occur within the demands of a National Curriculum. It means that teachers must find time to get together and plan for coherence and continuity of the learning from the student's perspective, whether this be between a secondary school's subject areas or from year to year in the primary school.

All this is no more than sound educational practice. Where such a marketing perspective goes beyond good current practice is its expectation that staff will enthuse about their work and the institution in which they deliver it externally, both formally through promotional events and informally through social and casual contacts.

Internal marketing also should address the work of non-teaching staff. The truculence of some school-keepers (caretakers) and the arrogance of some secretaries is part of the mythology of the staffroom. There are still, however, some grains of truth behind the crude stereotypes. Adult education classes are still terminated by the rattle of the caretaker's keys: telephone contacts with many educational organizations can be a lot less helpful than is now common in many commercial service organizations. This is in no way to criticize caretakers, receptionists or other support staff: the fault lies with institutional management – unless an internal marketing initiative has already been undertaken. All staff need information, skills and incentives if they are to maintain consistently an approach which places the customer first.

The infusion of such an attitude should start at the point where staff are first recruited. The procedures for recruiting staff should not be wholly separate from other aspects of the organization's marketing. Publicity materials to attract staff should be prepared with the same principles in mind as those prepared to recruit students, as discussed in the previous chapter. Advertising copy and the subsequent job details should be prepared so that the demands of the job are clearly spelled out in the job description and person specification, and the opportunities available to employees portrayed accurately and comprehensively. In particular, these should emphasize the service characteristics of the work, and the organization's commitment to a quality service and customer care. The skills involved in communicating with students and others need to feature significantly in the specifications for all posts involving customer contact. The importance, therefore, of drawing attention to such requirements as patience, flexibility and courtesy should not be overlooked: they may be obvious to the employer, but they may not be so obvious to those who, however qualified, have not worked previously in an organization committed to customer service.

The interviews and other recruitment techniques should similarly spell out the institution's commitment to its customers and the ways in which this is expressed in practical terms. They should look for evidence that this commitment will be shared by the successful candidate. Any concerns about this should be expressed in order to prepare an appropriate induction programme. That programme should be concerned substantially with enabling new employees to understand the central principles of a marketing-led approach, and to recognize the ways in which colleagues demonstrate these principles in their work.

Thereafter, the staff development programme can be used to assist staff to perceive students as customers, to understand why they are expected to behave in particular ways towards their customers, and to develop and enhance specific skills. These might include the skills required when dealing with face-to-face and telephone enquiries from potential customers, the skills needed for effective student support, including action planning and record-keeping, and those skills which ensure the success of promotional events such as open days. Such staff development is needed by both teaching and non-teaching staff. Although the distinction between these two groups might shape other staff development activities, it does not seem helpful or necessary here: joint staff development and training helps to underline the message that *all* staff have marketing responsibilities.

This message can be reinforced by the establishment of appropriate incentives and systems for staff motivation. Staff need to appreciate not just that they are required to undertake their work in particular ways. It is not even enough that they understand why they must work in these ways. They need to be rewarded for particular successes when applying these approaches. Some of the incentives used in other service industries, such as free holidays in the travel trade and cheap loans in the banks, are not available for the use of education managers. One reason for such incentives is that the staff can then talk knowledgeably about the service to potential customers. The offer of a place in a GCSE class to the school caretaker is not as obviously attractive as a free trip to Ibiza, although higher education institutions often offer free or discounted places on part-time programmes to both teaching and non-teaching staff.

Other devices, such as the familiar commercial ones of a suggestions box and cash rewards for staff whose suggestion are implemented, are employed in some educational organizations. They can stimulate staff to look for ways of enhancing quality and improving service. The pressures towards standardization of services are not so strong in most educational institutions as to institute staff uniforms and dress codes, although some head teachers do let their staff know what they regard as 'appropriate' dress, and at least one city technology college requires a staff uniform. Where a dress code is expected for pupils, staff need to reflect hard on the implications for them – what message does a male teacher with open neck shirt project to pupils who are required to wear ties? However, the conformity of dress expected in banks and hospitals is not usually sought in schools and colleges, where diversity of dress is often representative of the subject orientation of the teachers – sociology teachers are rarely as smartly turned out as business studies staff, while many art teachers demonstrate their creativity through their clothing, and physical education teachers wear tracksuits everywhere!

Some institutions now reward successful marketing activity directly, through the introduction of a commission system for successful student recruitment. The intensity of competition for overseas students means that many higher education establishments and some further education colleges now employ local agents in, for example, South-east Asia, who are paid a proportion of student fees for each student recruited through that agent.

MARKETING DIRECTOR:
c. £40,000 p.a. plus benefits

Middlesex Polytechnic is a leading centre of higher education with strong and established links with over 60 other European institutions.

Every year around 10,000 students at Middlesex Polytechnic take a whole range of courses from Accountancy to Zoology, and we enjoy a reputation as one of the most progressive and forward-thinking Polytechnics in the country.

We're now looking for an experienced marketing professional to join us as Marketing Director and bind together the promotional activities of our six Faculties and various other departments to form an integrated corporate marketing strategy for the Polytechnic as a whole.

We are committed to the effective promotion of the Polytechnic in order to generate the income and attract the investment that will facilitate even further development, continued growth, and ensure our position as a centre of excellence.

It is also vital that we continue to attract students to the full range of courses that we offer, and increase our involvement in research projects, consultancy work, and the provision of professional and vocational short courses for commerce and industry.

This is a position at the very highest level and we will look to you to identify new opportunities and initiate appropriate programmes to exploit them. As well as receiving the support of the present Head of Information Centre you will build and lead the marketing team to face this challenge.

As a member of the management team you will be working in close co-operation with the Deans of the Faculties and a broad range of staff involved in research, consultancy, short courses and a variety of services. You should be able to complement your expertise in external promotions with a flair for internal communications and the persuasive presentation skills to communicate aims and objectives.

Previous experience in the marketing of educational or training services is not essential. More important is the ability to demonstrate a sympathetic understanding of the relationship between our educational and commercial goals.

You will probably be educated to degree level and you must have a proven track record of effective marketing, from strategy development to the preparation of a broad range of promotional and publicity material. You should also be able to liaise with the news media in order to exploit public relations opportunities.

The salary for this position will be in the region of £40,000 and you can also look forward to a comprehensive benefits package that includes a performance related bonus, medical insurance, a fully expensed car and relocation assistance if appropriate.

Interviews will be held 9th and 10th October. Shortlisted candidates will be invited to tour the Polytechnic and meet potential senior colleagues prior to interview.

Please write, enclosing a full C.V. and covering letter, to Mike Bradley, Administration Director, (Ref: Mktng.), Middlesex Polytechnic, Queensway, Enfield, Middlesex EN3 4SF.

Closing date for applications: 21st September 1990.

Fig. 12   Rewarding the marketing manager: A recent job advertisement.

As student tuition fees for home-based students are pushed by the government nearer and nearer to the full costs, it may already be the case that some recruitment of home students is now undertaken on this commission basis; if not, it can't be long before it is introduced.

At the same time, performance-related pay is spreading through the education sectors, and student recruitment levels are important indicators of performance both for senior managers and for specialist marketing staff. Details of such arràngements are not normally openly disclosed, but some staff in public sector institutions now receive bonuses and salary increases, on the basis of their successes in boosting student recruitment or of winning substantial consultancy or research contracts. Until recently, this kind of incentive could only be achieved through the mechanisms of a 'college company'. The combination of delegated financial management and the gradual collapse of nationally established salary systems make this possible not only in colleges, universities and polytechnics. School governing bodies now have discretion as to the salary of the head teacher and deputy head: some are already using this discretion to reward recruitment success, now that student numbers are the paramount determinant of institutional income.

The concern for *quality* in education relates closely to the marketing perspective. One of the most potent approaches to quality improvement, labelled as 'total quality management', views people and teams within an organization as customers and suppliers of each other. Quality improvement is achieved by encouraging groups and individuals to examine and spell out their expectations of their suppliers and the requirements that customers have of them. In an educational organization, this blurs the distinctions between students and staff, looking instead at customers' needs and quality of service. The concept of 'internal marketing' similarly draws attention to the needs of both staff and students as customers. In seeking to improve the quality of service, all those involved in the quest for quality seek to promote customer care and enhance levels of satisfaction, whether the 'customers' are parents, students or colleagues in another section of the school or college department. The marketing strategies used to identify needs and to plan service delivery are as relevant to internal marketing as they are externally. The marketing perspective involves *everyone* in the organization.

9 | Organizing for marketing

This chapter falls into two distinct sections. The first looks at the management of the marketing function. The previous chapters have drawn attention to a long string of tasks and issues to be addressed by institutional managers when preparing and carrying out marketing strategies. In the first part of the chapter, these are drawn together, leading to proposals as to how marketing might most effectively be organized and managed. The starting point is the recognition of marketing as a key management responsibility. The associated management and leadership issues are examined with reference to planning, implementing and monitoring marketing performance. A specification of the range of tasks involved in marketing educational organizations is followed by an examination of the skills needed in order to undertake them effectively. Ways in which those marketing skills might be developed and enhanced are then explored. Alternative models for the organization of marketing in the different education sectors from primary schools to universities are considered, and proposals made. The organization of monitoring and evaluation is the last theme in this section.

The second part of the chapter looks at the tasks involved in the organization of income generation in educational organizations. Fund raising, trading activities and sponsorship are examined in turn, and special reference made to the organization of this aspect of an institution's work. Suggestions are made as to ways in which institutions might improve their income-generating activities, and integrate them as closely as possible with other areas of work.

Marketing and management

Marketing is a resource-consuming function, whose activities impinge directly upon the personnel, resource and curriculum management functions of any educational organization. These constitute senior management responsibilities, which might be undertaken individually or collectively within an organization. It is feasible, therefore, to identify marketing as a distinctive and specialist responsibility for a senior member of the institution's management team, or, given the all-pervading nature of a marketing perspective, for it to be the responsibility of all senior managers. If an organizational model involving collective responsibility is adopted, it is vital that all managers not only are aware of and in agreement with the marketing perspective underlying the institution's philosophy, but also have the necessary specialist marketing capabilities to be able to put that philosophy into practice successfully.

In seeking the appropriate location for marketing responsibilities, it is useful to look at the location of responsibilities for other key management functions. The most common and longest established differentiation between education management functions separates curriculum management from the other functions. Often these other functions are grouped together under a broad 'resource management' banner. Secondary schools have, for the past two decades, distinguished a 'pastoral management' function from the curriculum responsibilities, but this differentiation (probably arising initially out of the mergers between grammar schools and secondary modern schools and the need to find management work for senior secondary modern staff) is seen increasingly as not particularly appropriate. It separates two closely related aspects of a school's work while not being an accurate reflection of the range of management responsibilities to be undertaken within a senior management team.

The introduction of schemes for the 'local management' of schools and colleges has drawn sharper attention to two related resource management needs: finance management and personnel management. In larger institutions, senior appointments have been made with responsibility for each of these functions. At the same time, concern for quality and standards have led to the establishment of senior posts in further and higher education with specific and prime responsibility for 'academic standards' or 'quality control and assurance'.

In consequence, the appearance of marketing as a distinct management function means that it has to compete with the claims of other emergent areas of responsibility. This book has argued throughout for the significance of marketing as an *integrative* management function. Issues such as quality and standards can be subsumed under marketing (or vice versa). A distinction of some significance here, however, is that, while concepts of quality and standards are as all-pervasive as those of responsiveness and customer care, the marketing notions are backed by a well-tried and reasonably clearly defined body of knowledge and skills. In other words, as this book has tried to demonstrate, the appointment of a marketing manager suggests a more comprehensive, clear-cut and readily recognizable role specification than does the title of 'dean of academic standards' or 'deputy head teacher' (quality assurance).

This in itself is no strong argument for the appointment of a marketing manager at senior management team level. It does suggest, however, that in an organization committed to the improvement of quality, standards and responsiveness, two rather different qualities are needed. The first is an attribute of the chief executive (principal, head teacher, director, rector or vice-chancellor) in particular, and of senior managers in general. A passionate concern for quality improvement and customer interests does not necessarily have to be backed by a sophisticated array of marketing capabilities. It does need to recognize that these capabilities have to be well represented at a senior level in the organization, if that concern is to be translated into action. It follows that at least one of the senior managers must either come into the institution with those capabilities, or be prepared to invest considerable time, effort and energy in developing them.

The emergence of senior managers with marketing capabilities is a new phenomenon. Of course, many highly successful top education managers have been instinctively consummate marketeers, and have utilized a comprehensive range of marketing skills in developing their institutions both internally and externally. These skills have rarely been developed formally, nor sought formally when appointing the head teacher or principal. This is changing. Some experienced marketing managers are being attracted into education at a senior level as institutions now look for these particular qualities. However, as the book has tried to emphasize throughout, marketing skills are heavily context bound, so that their exercise in an educational context is all but impossible unless the person responsible has a thorough understanding of the educational market and its idiosyncracies as well as the organization, operation and politics of the education system. It is possible for an external consultant to advise on the management of finance and even on the application of personnel management policies, without knowing precisely and in detail the contexts in which the advice is to be applied; budgetary procedures and employment legislation are as applicable within schools as they are in factories and offices. It is much more difficult to recommend marketing strategies, unless the market and the organization's delivery capacity are understood intimately.

The emergence of a group of specialist marketing managers is most marked in the further education sector. Response to the criticisms of the sector's lack of responsiveness and the readiness of the Manpower Services Commission/Training Agency to encourage marketing by funding research and supporting specialist marketing appointments within colleges has led to the appointment of marketing officers in most colleges. These still tend to be part-time rather than full-time appointments in the smaller colleges, where marketing the college may be timetabled for some 20–50 percent of an enthusiast's timetable. In consequence, that person's working week becomes longer and longer, until the pressures cause the marketeer to move to a post where marketing is a full-time responsibility. There are dangers that the marketing officer becomes overloaded with a host of instant crises and odd jobs. Walker and Hooper (1988) and Scribbins and Davies (1989) have in different ways looked at appropriate roles for marketing managers and appropriate organizational structures for colleges. The enormous potential workloads for marketeers makes it essential that both the roles of marketing staff and their place within the organizational structure are clearly defined.

Post-school institutions are likely to require at least one full-time marketing appointment, to be supported appropriately in terms of both physical resources (budget, secretarial support, etc.) and of organizational authority. Thus the 'red guard' approach of using an enthusiastic junior member of staff in a part-time marketing post to attack traditional attitudes and institute radically new approaches is being replaced by the appointment of increasingly senior managers at assistant and vice-principal levels with overall marketing responsibilities. These posts are then backed by specialist staff with responsibility for some of the tasks itemized at the beginning of this chapter – industrial liaison, schools liaison, publicity/graphic design and media relations.

However, in many organizations, and particularly in higher education, appointments have been made on a piecemeal basis as needs have arisen. Poor media relations in the past have encouraged a number of polytechnics to appoint information or public relations officers. School liaison and industrial liaison appointments have been made to stimulate recruitment – and often where a department's decline has made a member of staff surplus to requirements but too talented to make redundant. The opportunities presented by Europe and for overseas student recruitment have led to further *ad hoc* appointments.

In secondary schools, marketing responsibilities tend to be distributed among the 'pastoral' staff, with the head of first year liaising with feeder primary schools and so responsible for recruitment. In both primary and secondary schools, the head teacher usually takes direct responsibility for public relations and commonly for recruitment. Budgets do not allow for specialist appointments at any level, and in consequence staff development in order to enhance marketing skills is particularly important here.

Marketing tasks

A checklist of the major marketing tasks to be undertaken in most educational organizations includes:

- liaison with feeder institutions;
- organizing student recruitment;
- overseas student recruitment;
- employer/industrial/commercial liaison;
- fund raising and sponsorship;
- promoting, costing and organizing income-generating activities including lettings and short courses;
- media relations and public relations;
- preparation of brochures and other publicity materials;
- European Community issues;
- marketing research;

- preparing marketing plans;
- managing 'front-of-house' environment, reception and other customer contact;
- quality assurance, monitoring and customer care;
- after-sales services, including alumni liaison; and
- organizing related staff development and training activities.

These tasks can be divided into five or six categories, distinguished by the differences both in the work to be undertaken and the skills needed to do this work. One way of distinguishing these is to differentiate between:

- the research, analysis and planning tasks;
- the recruitment tasks, involving liaison with feeder institutions and the organization of promotional activities and publicity, together with reception and other customer contact responsibilities;
- the income-generation tasks, involving fund raising and sponsorship, and the development of income-generating activities including lettings and short courses;
- employer/industrial/commercial liaison, which might include both commercial sponsorship and some aspects of recruitment as well as student placement;
- the informational tasks involved in designing and preparing publicity and informational materials, together with media and public relations;
- after-sales services, including alumni liaison; and
- the internal marketing tasks, including staff development, customer care and monitoring and evaluation.

An institution may seek to concentrate some or all of these tasks in the job description of one individual 'marketing manager', to distribute them among a marketing team, or to expect all managers – or at least senior managers – to take on these responsibilities. The organizational consequences of distinguishing between marketing tasks in this way are examined below, as are the skills required in order to undertake these tasks effectively.

Marketing skills

Educational managers with marketing responsibilities need an extensive portfolio of skills and techniques if they are to work effectively. These include:

1. A knowledge of and the relevant skills in the main techniques of marketing research, information analysis and forecasting, both for predicting future needs and for estimating their impact on (and ways in which they might be met by) educational organizations.
2. Recognition of the different perceptions of the education service and specific institutions within it by employers, employees, students and parents; along with variations in perceptions relating to gender, race, culture and social class, and the consequences of such perceptions on demands for particular forms of educational provision.
3. The marketing and management skills necessary to organize effective planning and promotional activities.
4. The ability to analyse an organization in political terms, identifying power and influence and the objectives of key political actors; together with the political skills needed to operate effectively in that environment, to obtain and exercise power and to influence others.
5. The abilities needed to motivate colleagues, to develop marketing perspectives and philosophies, and to organize appropriate forms of training and development.
6. Judgements and insights of sufficient quality to enable them to integrate marketing as both a philosophy and a management function throughout the organization.

If marketing managers are to contribute usefully to the development of their institution's services, they must understand and be involved in the institutional processes through which things get done. This means operating through the formal arenas of senior management team meetings, academic board meetings, staff meetings and working parties. Experience from colleges and polytechnics suggests that marketing managers are often handicapped in these procedures by their relative inexperience of institutional politics and by the fact that their work takes them out of the institution for much of their time, so that they do not recognize until it is too late that political processes are operating against them. They find it hard to fulfil that Victorian recipe for political success – 'Be present!' In one of the few research investigations of the work of educational marketing managers, Gray and Williams (1990) found that marketing managers recognized that they were disadvantaged in the institutional power struggles which affected their work, but rarely had the skills or the resources to be able to act effectively in those struggles.

Those with marketing responsibilities need to recognize that schools and colleges are political organizations, and that many of those who operate most effectively therein do so by creating and maintaining the illusion that power and politics have no place in educational institutions. Political activity is not a symptom of organizational sickness, but rather one of democratic health. And educational institutions can only provide adequate preparation for a democratic society if they operate as good working examples of democratic organizations.

The tools and techniques needed for effective operation in the political arena are probably at least as useful as techniques for sophisticated technical analysis, when trying to influence the organization and delivery of services in an educational organization. The effective marketeer needs a sound understanding of the school or college as a political arena. Knowledge of the institution's political history and past battles – attempts to close down courses, establish new ones, change organizational structures – is needed. It is necessary to understand the power resources of the different groups within the organization, and the bases of their legitimacy, using the analyses outlined in Chapter 4. Key questions from this perspective are likely to include the following. Are the professional associations organized effectively? Do some departments hold more power than others, and why? Which of the non-teaching staff influence the school's politics and how?

Marketeers need political skills in order to operate effectively in this environment. These include the ability to identify clear and realistic objectives, to obtain support for those objectives by forming alliances and coalitions, then to mount campaigns through the formal and informal organizational structures in pursuit of those objectives, to be able to bargain with and negotiate compromises with those opposing the campaign by recognizing clearly the objectives of those in opposition, and to come to and be able to deliver agreements which meet at least partially the objectives of those involved – and it means having trusted allies who provide cover and intelligence when the marketeer is working outside the institution.

Developing marketing managers

Staff development and formal training in marketing skills is now beginning to be made available for education managers. As might be expected, the further education sector responded first. The

Training Agency-funded Responsive College Programme (Theodossin, 1989) has already been referred to. It has published a substantial pack of training materials, including three video-cassettes, as a basis for training both specialist marketing staff and all staff who come into contact with students and other customers. The intention has been that these should be used by colleges for their in-house staff development and training activities.

For the past 5 years, The Staff College, (formerly the Further Education Staff College: the only national education management centre in the UK and base for the Responsive College Programme) has offered short courses in educational marketing to managers in further, higher and adult education. Arising from these courses, a national organization for educational marketing managers has been established, The Marketing Network, with its office at the Polytechnic of East London. This now has an institutional membership of over 200 colleges, and at the time of writing is active in organizing a national 'Further Education Week' in order to promote the benefits available from this sector. Marketing Network activities also include national conferences and regional events organized through a regional network, which offer opportunities for staff development.

Opportunities for the more substantial development of educational marketing skills are also now available for all sectors. Several higher education institutions, including the University of Manchester and the Polytechnic of East London, have introduced specialist options on their management training diplomas in education management, and a recent CNAA review of education management provision found that they have been emulated by a number of institutions. The short courses at The Staff College can now be linked together with distance learning units from Henley: The Management College to lead to a Diploma in Education Management (validated by Brunel University: an interesting and quite complex example of a franchising arrangement in higher education). There is also a specialist post-experience BTEC module in educational marketing.

As a result of these developments, it is now becoming possible for education managers to develop and enhance their marketing skills, not only through practical management experience but also through a variety of training opportunities. These seem likely to encourage the development of a cadre of 'home-grown' education marketing managers, who move into marketing from teaching and education administration, rather than for institutions and local authorities to have to seek marketeers from outside the education service for senior marketing posts. This should offer encouragement to those who look with some concern at the experience of other public services such as the NHS, when managers from industry and commerce inexperienced in the needs and ways of the NHS have been recruited.

Organizational tasks and structures

Organizational models for educational institutions are influenced first by the size of the institution, and hence the capacity to be able to employ specialists in the areas defined in the task specification defined earlier, and, secondly, by the institution's mission and its need for a number of dedicated marketing specialists in order to accomplish that mission.

The organizational location of the marketing function in further and higher education organizations has been discussed by Scribbins and Davies (1989). They emphasize that the marketing function is a key aspect of management, and examine the disadvantages of the 'sub-management model', whereby relatively junior staff are given responsibility for an organization's marketing. They also point to an emergent 'general and lieutenant's model', whereby the advantages of institutional collaboration are enhanced by the LEA-wide organization of marketing under an LEA marketing co-ordinator. Megson (1988) provides some practical demonstrations of this approach.

In smaller organizations, it is more likely that the marketing tasks are brought together in one or two persons, so that, in primary schools, it is most likely to be the head teacher who takes direct responsibility for the school's marketing internally and externally. This has the virtues of integrating all the management tasks; it has the disadvantage of requiring that one person have the capabilities required for resource, personnel and curriculum management as well as marketing.

A large institution such as a university, polytechnic or large college could well bring these responsibilities together under a member of the senior management team, with direct responsibility for the organization of marketing research and the preparation of marketing plans, together with the management of ethos and environment, organizing related staff development and training activities, and the quality assurance and monitoring tasks required to ensure high service standards (although these latter might be brought together in a separate 'quality assurance' post). This post could be supported by specialist staff with specific responsibilities for the tasks specified earlier – planning and research, recruitment, income generation, employer liaison, information and internal marketing. The income generation tasks might be subdivided further with separate offices for alumni liaison, overseas student affairs and European issues.

In some further and higher education institutions, some or all of the income-generating tasks are undertaken within a 'college company', established to undertake some or all of the income-generation tasks indicated above. The Further Education Act 1985 encouraged the establishment and use of such companies, and TRACE (1986) gave advice as to how such companies might be established and managed. After the Education Reform Act 1988 extended the powers of colleges to undertake trading activities, the advantages of separate companies are less obvious, and some disadvantages have become apparent. In particular, the relationship between the company, its board of directors and the 'parent' institution has been strained where the profit-making purposes of the company have not coincided with the college's mission or current priorities. The management and organization of the company, and the tasks undertaken by the company's management, need to be specified clearly, and as clearly differentiated from the tasks undertaken within the parent organization. Technical issues concerning the payment of value-added tax, the reward systems used for college employees who also work for the company, professional indemnity insurance and intellectual property rights, all need to be resolved if college companies are to operate effectively in support of their parent institutions.

In many educational organizations, public relations is subsumed within the broader marketing responsibilities, and only larger institutions can afford a specialist appointment here. The responsibilities include the provision of information about the organization (the person responsible for PR in some educational establishments is called the 'information officer') and responsibilities for liaison with the media.

Evaluating marketing

Education managers must look at the effectiveness of their marketing decisions, including fund-raising decisions. Evaluative and

monitoring techniques are needed, which should ensure that marketing plans are being implemented as intended. The analytical
techniques recommended in Chapter 4 can provide a starting
point. It is important to emphasize that monitoring and evaluation
should be considered as part of the planning processes, and the
procedures for marketing audit and marketing research provide a
starting point for the collection and analysis of relevant evidence.
The systems for collecting and using such evidence need to be in
place as soon as the marketing plan starts to be put into practice.

Institutions need to know the answers to a number of questions
about their marketing. These include:

- Which marketing objectives are and are not being achieved?
- How satisfied are customers (and their sponsors) about the recruitment procedures, the service delivery, and the after-sales
  services, including the extent to which anticipated benefits have
  been obtained?
- How much is being spent on all aspects of marketing?
- What returns are being achieved from that expenditure?
- Which marketing activities produce the most and the least
  returns?
- How might more, less or different ways of investing in marketing produce different returns?
- Does the institution have the most appropriate organizational
  structure to manage its marketing?
- How are marketing objectives, strategies and successes being
  communicated to staff?
- How are staff contributing to the improvement of the institu-
  tion's services and marketing approaches?
- How might the marketing planning and marketing research processes be improved?

The questions themselves need to be asked in a structured and
organized way, so that the answers can be used both in the market
strategy's regular fine-tuning needed throughout the year and in
the cyclical evaluation in preparation for the next marketing plan.
There is a good deal of information available around any educational organization, and it is not proposed here that yet another
time-consuming set of questionnaires or other surveys be in-
stituted. Rather, institutions should look hard at the existing
sources of information and see whether they can be so organized
as to provide appropriate marketing information. A study of the

work of college marketing officers (Gray and Williams, 1990) found that college management information systems (MIS) did not contain the sorts of information useful to marketing officers, but that the officers did not want to set up new marketing information systems – they wanted the existing MIS to be improved and readily available.

Those with marketing responsibilities need to be consulted in order to recommend ways in which the existing systems can be improved. These are likely to include not only the school or college MIS – now likely to be all the more important because of financial delegation and the outcomes of staff appraisal policies. The staff appraisal procedures in any institution committed to quality and customer service would normally include some investigation of staff perceptions of institutional service, quality and responsiveness, and ways in which staff have made and might make contributions to their improvement. Sensitivity is needed in both collecting and making use of such information, and few UK institutions would want to take up Kotler and Fox's (1985) suggestion that individual staff members be rated according to their fund-raising effectiveness. However, the appraisal system might be a vehicle both for identifying significant staff contributions to marketing improvement and for taking steps whereby such contributions might be rewarded.

A final point. The collection and analysis of monitoring and evaluative evidence needs to be built into the work of those with marketing responsibilities, and the procedures whereby the outcomes of such analysis be used to improve the organization's effectiveness need to be spelled out clearly, so that all staff are able to recognize when proposals and actions are based on evidence rather than whim and are designed to improve institutional performance. This comes back to a point emphasized in Chapter 8: those holding such responsibilities and required to take such actions also need to be given sufficient authority to ensure that the actions *will* be taken and the improvements made.

Fund raising

Virtually all educational institutions are now under pressure to obtain resources through their own efforts. Public sector institutions are exhorted to reduce their dependence upon public funds by generating income. A decade of financial stringency has accustomed education managers to recognize that the gap between what they believe they need and what the government will provide is steadily widening, so that they must choose between making do with less or raising funds to bridge that gap. The decline in total student numbers has aggravated the funding problem. As institutions have become smaller, a higher proportion of their resources has been consumed by the fixed costs required just to keep the place open. Although government figures show that spending on a per capita basis has increased, this is not reflected at institutional level, where the amount available after fixed costs have been met has bought less and less each year.

Until recently, fund raising activities in UK schools were undertaken in order to raise money for 'extras', those items which the local authority could not be expected to provide: a mini-bus or a swimming pool for a secondary school; playground equipment or a football strip for the primary school. This has changed. Schools now depend upon private funds for the basics of education – textbooks, computers and stationery. This has been endorsed officially: when the Department of Trade and Industry made funds available for computers in primary and secondary schools, it required that half of the cost be found by the schools themselves – and for most schools that could only be achieved through fund raising.

The high levels of competence and ingenuity of education managers as resource managers has been recognized when compared with private sector organizations (Torrington and Weightman, 1989). They have become expert in achieving a great deal with remarkably limited resources. It is not surprising, therefore, that this ingenuity has been extended to the mobilization of additional resources. This is being undertaken in three rather different ways: begging, trading and sponsorship. Each is considered in turn.

Begging has a long tradition in education. The precursors of our schools and universities were founded by enthusiasts who begged neighbours and businesses for 'subscriptions', and the service has always depended to some extent upon the goodwill and generosity of responses to such appeals. The appeals are not necessarily for cash. Further education colleges successfully scrounge machinery and equipment from local manufacturers; primary schools beg for furniture, paper and carpets. Special schools are particularly successful, in that they attract support from every quarter, including other schools and colleges.

The approaches spelled out elsewhere in the book apply to the organization of fund raising. It is vital first to understand the market, then to identify appropriate market segments, and then to plan and organize an effective marketing campaign. Four distinct market segments are examined next: former students (alumni), charitable trusts, industry and commerce, and the local community.

Organized begging from former students takes place most successfully in higher education, where graduates and diplomats are sought out and asked to show their appreciation of their 'Alma Mater' by joining and then regularly contributing through an 'alumni association'. This is a US model, developed in an education system which has never been as heavily dependent upon public funds as the UK systems. It has been employed for many years by older UK universities and is now being developed in the polytechnics and colleges.

The development of alumni associations is an indication that fund raising is becoming more organized in the UK. In the past, specific appeals were made when institutions faced financial crises. Now a continuing fund-raising function is established and maintained, to ensure that funds are obtained all the time rather than on special occasions. Fund raising is now such an important part of the work of the larger US colleges and universities, that it has required the establishment of 'development offices' with a number of full-time staff specializing in particular donor groups such as charitable trusts, corporations and private donors. These are backed by carefully marshalled cohorts of volunteers, as is described by Kotler and Fox (1985). The larger UK higher education institutions are now approaching this level of investment in fund raising. The University of Oxford attracted headlines when it appointed a full-time fund raiser in 1988, publicity which immediately went some way to justify the cost of the investment. The 'Campaign for Oxford' raised over a quarter of its £220 million target in its first year (and attracted a lot of criticism that it was diverting donations away from worthier causes). It approached this by building a data bank of the university's 150000 graduates, and employing a large team of professional fund raisers. As this demonstrates, a major campaign can be expensive: an investment of 10 percent of the target sought is generally seen as the minimum needed for a successful fund-raising campaign.

A well-organized fund-raising system relies upon extensive and regularly updated data banks on former graduates, built from as many possible sources as possible, including regular scanning of the business press and social news – and including, in US universities, details of property holdings, legal and probate decisions, marriages and divorces. As a result, when a particularly large injection of funds is required, for a new library or residential block, the organization exists to reach out rapidly into alumni pockets.

A further feature of the more organized approach is that something is provided in return for their contributions. Membership of an alumni association is marketed as a benefit, where the association brings graduates together for social events and where overseas students are put in touch with each other through the association. Other 'benefits' are even more obvious. In Thailand, the names and portraits of a school's benefactors are painted on to the school wall, along with the total number of Bahts contributed.

The nation's charitable trusts, many of which were established specifically for educational purposes, are obvious but relatively unexploited targets for organized begging campaigns. The private schools have long been adept in exploiting these resources, but they can also be approached by public sector institutions. Research is required to discover possible charities. The annual guides such as the *Directory of Grant-Making Trusts* and the *Charities Digest* give information about both the major charities and the strategies needed in order to submit an application. But there are many local charities which are not included in the guides, and personal investigation may be necessary to reveal their existence and their current priorities. It is also possible for parents' associations to establish their own charities for the benefit of the school. Covenant schemes then enable schools to reclaim the tax paid on parental contributions covenanted to the school.

Industry and commerce are constantly being exhorted to augment government funding by making donations to education, the arts and other services supported traditionally by government. Educational institutions are rapidly improving their links with local industry and commerce, not least because of the recent eruption of business representatives on to school and college governing bodies. Apart from cash donations, industry commonly provides redundant machinery and equipment to schools and further education colleges. Examples range from a solicitor's firm giving a photocopier to a primary school, to an engineering firm transferring its equipment to the local further education college after installing upgraded equipment. Some of the nation's best-known names now fund a wide range of initiatives in every sector of the education service. The major oil companies and retail chains have been active in providing not only financial help but also valuable expertise in the form of free consultancy advice and the attachment of managers to a local education authority or a college. It is increasingly common for managers to be seconded in this way, either shortly before their retirement or as a means for broadening a high-flying manager's experience. Gorman (1988) offers sensible advice on ways in which schools and colleges might approach both business organizations and charitable trusts.

The local community has traditionally been the mainstay of support for primary and secondary schools, and most schools have well-established systems for tapping this support through fund-raising activities. These have usually operated at arm's length from the school, through a Parent–Teacher Association (PTA) or 'Friends of the School', with the consequence that the purposes of such fund raising may also be determined outside the school, and there have been examples of PTAs spending money on items not sought by the school – such as a set of mathematics textbooks which provided a more traditional approach than the approach favoured by the primary school head teacher. It is important, therefore, that the school is represented on the PTA committees, and that staff are encouraged to involve themselves with PTA activities, to ensure that the organization does not become too distant from the school and its needs. However, many schools would not be able to offer the level of service they achieve, were it not for the efforts and hard work of the PTA.

Most schools also raise funds directly, operating a 'school fund' quite separate from the funds provided by the LEA or central government. It is only recently that schools have been required to reveal to parents and LEAs the existence of these funds and to publish annual accounts. Gray (1984) has analysed the ways in which one primary school raises funds both directly and through the PTA, and then spends those funds. LEA restrictions on ways in which these funds might be used have now been lifted under local management schemes. Previously, some local authorities prohibited certain forms of expenditure such as buying-in extra teaching help.

Fund-raising events demonstrate the need both for organization and for contributors to be wooed by being offered something in return for their generosity. Gorman (1988) notes that schools raised over £70 million in extra funds in 1987, and offers advice on a wide range of strategies which might be used by schools to boost their resources.

An organized approach to fund raising involves both careful planning and an understanding of marketing strategies, using principles expounded throughout this book. There are now so many competing demands for money from the general public that educational institutions must do more than beg blatantly for help if they are to raise funds successfully. They need to recognize that benefits must be demonstrated. These may be benefits to the children and grandchildren of those approached for help. This involves the clear specification of targets for fund-raising campaigns – a strategy long employed by schools working through their Parent–Teacher Associations, when they have specified, say, new gymnasium equipment or library books as the target for particular fund-raising activities.

The benefits might be aimed directly at the donors, in the form of an enjoyable social occasion, e.g. a dance, bingo session or excursion. Or they might be the prospect of financial benefit from a tombola, lottery, raffle or '100 Club' (in which a proportion of an annual membership subscription is put aside for money prizes at a monthly draw).

The most valuable source of community support – at least in primary schools – is the free help given by parents and others who come into schools regularly to work in classrooms, assist with clerical work and contribute directly to the teaching processes. In a sector committed to individualized approaches to learning, many teachers would not be able to operate effectively if it were not for this regular assistance. As with other forms of help, this needs careful planning and forethought in order to make the fullest use of these valuable resources to the benefit of the pupils.

One further source of substantial additional support for some institutions should be noted: the Department of Education and Science. Observers long used to the limited resources of this small government department and the problems involved in extracting funds therefrom have been astonished at the ways in which it has been able to support generously in both cash and kind first city technology colleges and then grant-maintained schools. It has stepped into the breach caused when commercial sponsors failed to appear in sufficient numbers to support the city technology colleges, providing cash and free professional advice from its Architects and Buildings Department and elsewhere. Then local authorities were surprised to see the extent to which the capital building programmes of schools who had 'opted out' of local authority control were supported by the DES – almost as though only those schools in the final stages of dereliction had chosen to opt for grant maintained status.

Trading activities are commonplace in schools and colleges. Here, those services which are neither directly educational (courses, research, consultancy) nor undertaken as part and in support of the educational processes (training restaurants and mini-businesses) are examined.

In higher education, the students' union undertakes a wide range of trading activities from shops to bars and cafes, sometimes in competition with the facilities provided by the institution. The operation of trading activities in colleges was commonly on a subsidized or cost-recovery basis until recently. There is now pressure to produce surpluses and a contribution to the institution's overall running costs. The organization of the provision of food and drink is being scrutinized carefully in many institutions. Monitoring procedures tailor provision more carefully to customer demands, while space utilization studies help to find ways to improve through-put and to speed up service. The use of automated food and drink dispensing equipment reduces labour costs and ensures surpluses if hire charges are related to a percentage of sales.

Schools and colleges also generate income by selling personalized mementos such as individual and class photographs, video- and audio-cassettes of special events, concerts and leaving ceremonies, magazines and other publications, as well as personalized souvenirs, badges and items of clothing. The organization of sales points needs careful scrutiny to ensure that total costs – calculated to include time involved in buying in stock, commissioning suppliers, staffing the sales point and managing cash and accounts – are not to exceed income received.

Commercially attractive non-educational ventures include the use of space for car-parking where the institution is attractively located near a city centre or sporting stadium. Car boot sales are a currently fashionable additional opportunity for renting school or college space, whether these are organized by the institution or the space rented to a commercial provider. The sale of advertising space in school and college publications and brochures is becoming an increasingly significant source of revenue, while the collection of materials for recycling both provides some funds and engages students in activities with environmental benefits.

The school and college premises generate further income. Classrooms and halls are let in the evenings and at weekends for recreational and adult education purposes to voluntary organizations like The Women's Institute and private organizations such as dance schools and bridge clubs. Until recently, these lettings were commonly offered as a free or low-cost community service. Increasingly, governing bodies are requiring that they are undertaken on an income-generating basis, so that the returns do more than just cover the costs of the caretaking and cleaning staff. Bingo and bridge sessions, often organized by the Parent–Teacher Association in the evenings, and wedding receptions, discos and parties at weekends provide further income. Schools and colleges have become small or medium-sized businesses – and have in consequence begun to experience some of the problems faced by such businesses, ranging from value-added tax returns to cash-flow problems, stock management and unpaid bills. It is vital that such trading enterprises are established from the outset on a sound business footing, with proper management. School and college managers should heed and learn from the difficulties faced by many student unions, as they expanded their trading activities some years ago.

Sponsorship is a distinctive form of income generation with elements of both begging and trading. The targets are usually private sector organizations who provide financial support in return for advertising that support and their products on educational materials, equipment and publications. Staff posts have long been supported by sponsors: Archbishop Laud sponsored Oxford's Laudian Chair of Arabic in 1640. Most higher education institutions now seek commercial sponsorship both for fully funded professorial posts, and for top-up funding which will attract applicants to posts paid substantially above the normal rate for the job. It is common for major educational conferences to be supported by a collection of commercial and governmental organizations, who then advertise their beneficence on the conference brochures and stationery. School exercise books are now emblazoned with the name of the sponsor, and Oxbridge colleges have advertised the names of their founders since the middle ages. University libraries, residential blocks and laboratories are also named after their benefactors, and it can only be a matter of time before schools and colleges modify their names to incorporate that of the sponsor.

In seeking institutional sponsorship, schools and colleges need to consider whether an exclusive sponsorship arrangement is sought, whereby an educational institution or event is 'branded' as being sponsored by one organization whose name is then clearly associated with that event or place; or whether multiple sponsorship is sought, with contributions from a range of organizations. It is often more attractive from the sponsor's point of view, especially for an event such as a prestigious conference, for an exclusive arrangement which demonstrates the beneficence of the single sponsor. The organization must be sure that not only will the funding cover the amount needed in total – which means that this needs to be carefully estimated in advance of seeking sponsorship – but that the close association with one business enterprise will not have any deleterious consequences: likely sources of sponsorship are commonly producers of products with which a school or college might not want to be too obviously or closely associated, such as alcohol or tobacco. Sleight (1990) offers advice on seeking sponsorship which can be adapted to educational contexts.

Another form of sponsorship, of increasing significance as commercial organizations recognize the significance for their own activities of the falling numbers of young people entering the job market, is the sponsorship of individual students. Some parts of higher education have long received such sponsorship, notably with competitive bursaries for students on engineering courses, and some companies have long sponsored the children of senior employees while at school and college. These approaches are now being extended to the school sector, with the offer of 2-year bursaries, worth from £100 to £500 per year, for some sixth formers. In return, the sponsored students will undertake paid work for their sponsors during the school holidays. The marketing opportunities of this form of sponsorship are for institutions or particular departments to encourage students to come to them because of the access they offer to student bursaries. Concerns have been expressed that these amount to 'bribes' to encourage students and parents to switch schools.

Organizing for fund raising

Fund raising usually forms part of the responsibilities of the marketing or public relations unit in larger organizations and the head teacher or principal in smaller establishments. Professional fund-raising consultants are now actively seeking business in the education sectors, although they have long been employed by private schools. It is important to recognize when considering buying this form of commercial assistance that not only are there the direct costs of the consultant, but to these must be added the staff time and school resources needed in order to work with and carry out the recommendations of the consultant. Professional fund raisers do not go off quietly and come back with briefcases full of cheques. They work closely with the school or college staff, helping them to set objectives and undertake strategies in order to meet those objectives. In other words, they help schools organize themselves more efficiently. Institutions must estimate all of these costs, and need to be confident that returns will comfortably exceed the necessary investment before bringing in such external help.

As with other aspects of marketing, an organized approach to fund raising is essential. This requires careful planning and an understanding of marketing approaches, backed by an appropriate organizational structure. The basic steps needed in organizing fund raising are those propounded throughout this book. Fund raising needs proper planning, and must be organized as a part of the broader marketing activities of the institution. It is vital first to examine and set realistic objectives and turn these into cash targets. It is then necessary to look hard at the market, to identify appropriate market segments, and then to plan and organize an effective marketing campaign. This includes the recognition that benefits need to be demonstrated and that the institution needs to be capable of delivering those benefits. It involves thorough marketing research in order to identify opportunities, and the clear identification of the institution's strengths and weaknesses in mounting a fund-raising campaign. 'Threats' need to be identified, including the legal constraints and requirements to be heeded.

The marketing research should lead to the establishment of an information system in which categories of funding sources – former students, charities, corporate donors, community sources, corporate sponsors, trading ventures – are recorded and their characteristics noted. A fund-raising strategy can then be planned in which each of the elements of the 'mix' are appraised. In particular, the investment of financial and human resources in fund-raising activities needs careful scrutiny. It requires clear-sighted objectives if resources provided for educational purposes are to be diverted in order to attract additional resources. Options need to be explored and opportunity costs considered, before deciding whether to boost an institution's trading activities or to use the time and money to mount a campaign to attract sponsors. An important aspect of the marketing mix to be considered here is the attitudes and interests of the staff to be involved in fund raising. Staff are commonly invited and even expected to give voluntarily of their time in the evenings and at weekends to support fund raising, whether it be staffing a white elephant stall at the summer fair, working out the accounts for the school tuck-shop or addressing former students at an alumni association meeting. Their money might even be sought for lottery tickets, '100 Club' membership or tombola prizes. Teachers and non-teaching staff might look around in vain for other areas of employment where employees are expected to give up their spare time and money to help their employer make ends meet. In view of this, it is surprising that so many staff are still willing to help out in the ways that they do. It is crucial that this commitment is recognized, and that such recognition extends to the involvement of contributors in decisions both about the objectives to be achieved from fund raising and the strategies to be adopted. A research study some years ago in primary schools found that schools where staff participated in deciding how non-LEA funds should be spent were more successful in raising funds than those where the head made the decisions (Gray, 1983). The procedures for allocating resources provided by the government may not be appropriate for allocating the returns from fund-raising activities, even where those resources are needed for essentials.

In referring to the planning of fund raising, warnings should also be given about the constraints which must be taken into account before embarking on a planned activity. These range from the need for licences in order to provide either live or recorded music and to sell alcohol, to the requirements of legislation concerning health and safety and gambling activities such as lotteries, and the need to consider contingency plans and insurance. Trading activities might invite complaints from local businesses about unfair competition, while the generation of surpluses or 'profits' can make an institution liable to tax on these profits.

The generation of additional resources requires, therefore, clear objectives, the precise targeting of market segments and meticulous planning. The community which might respond warmly and generously to a regular bridge club at the school may show no interest in weekly bingo sessions. The familiar spring fêtes, summer fairs and Christmas entertainments need to be undertaken with a clear understanding of their purpose – whether to publicize the school's contributions to the community, to involve pupils in community-related activity or to make money. If the latter is the prime objective, these events may be less effective in achieving that objective than the investment of time and other resources in rather different money-making activities.

The planning of fund-raising activities requires recognition that this *consumes* resources, particularly staff time, but also publicity costs and the expenditure necessary for events, ranging from an appearance fee to a local or national celebrity to the provision of prizes, food and drink and items for sale. The concept of opportunity costs is important here. Before making a commitment to a specific fund-raising event, the costs in cash and human resources need to be estimated and the question asked as to whether these resources might be more effectively deployed in a different way. Education managers also need to consider the costs of heavy staff involvement in fund-raising activities in terms of their prime task, their teaching work. The organization of such events is very time-consuming and it would be ironic if the students for whose benefits the resources were being generated were in fact to suffer because of the diversion of staff energies to the fund-raising work.

10 | An emerging marketing perspective

This final chapter looks at some of the practical problems involved when attempting to improve the marketing of educational organizations, starting with the problems of applying a marketing perspective in a centrally controlled educational system, exploring issues of collaboration and competition between institutions. Finally, an indigenous approach to educational marketing is proposed, built on sound educational practice, in which a marketing perspective is recognized as a reinforcement of well-established student-centred approaches, albeit with an injection of new skills and strategies.

Marketing in an imperfect market

Market forces have never been allowed to operate freely in government-funded education services, and government interference with such forces is more marked today than it has ever been, despite current rhetoric. Educational institutions are being exhorted to market themselves with one hand tied behind their backs and both feet firmly chained to separate stakes labelled 'Department of Education and Science' and 'Department of Employment'.

A marketing perspective in public sector education has to take account of the imperfect market. A healthy democratic society demonstrates its health in part by the interest it shows in the performance and quality of its vital public services. This is reflected by governmental scrutiny and regulation of the education service. It is not enough, however, for educational organizations to depend upon that regulation in order to contain the potential dangers of a free-market economy. A marketing perspective must contain centrally within it the clear recognition that the public service should be available to satisfy the needs of all its publics. This includes those groups traditionally disadvantaged in their access to high-quality education. Marketing is a vital means by which such groups are first made aware of the opportunities available to them, and then helped to make full use of the services thus provided. Any equal opportunities policy must have a marketing dimension – and vice versa.

Similarly, a marketing perspective should not disadvantage some institutions and their members because of the superior marketing skills of a rival organization. A marketing perspective must check the impulse towards destructive forms of inter-institutional competition, and encourage the identification of ways in which institutions might more effectively collaborate locally and regionally. The dangers of a highly competitive market economy have been spelled out by Finegold and Soskice (1988) and others. They have contrasted the poor performance of economies, such as those of the UK and the USA, in which fierce competition has led to cost-cutting, low investment in education and training, and in consequence poorly skilled workers producing low-quality goods and services. This is contrasted with the performance of economies with a 'high-skill equilibrium', where association and specialization are more important than competition. There is, therefore, more scope for investment in high technology and training, leading to high-quality goods and services, produced by highly skilled employees. Educational organizations need to look at the advantages of specialization and of association and collaboration with each other, rather than waste their resources in cut-throat competition. Marketing then draws attention to the quality of the specialist services and the ways in which a complex service can be obtained from several organizations working in association with each other. In some areas, schools have banded together in order to promote collectively their service; for example, Avon's secondary schools have hired a public relations agency to help them promote their strengths, including the ways in which schools cooperate to improve their service through consortia.

The National Association of Head Teachers (1990) has published a code of conduct for all its members, to encourage such
collaboration. This defines and seeks to proscribe 'unprofessional
activities', such as the offer of inducements (e.g. gifts and commercial incentives to prospective pupils), the reporting of examination
results in ways which undermine rival schools, and the use of
money from teaching funds on marketing activities. The code
states that its members should take account of the effects of their
marketing activities on neighbouring schools.

Local authorities have shown similar concerns that marketing
does not degenerate into destructive competition. Warwickshire
has published a voluntary code of conduct for its schools which
proposes constraints upon the distribution of publicity materials,
and strongly discourages any comparisons between schools,
whether in publicity materials and advertising or in public
meetings.

Home-grown educational marketing

The argument that a marketing perspective needs to infuse all
educational organizations and involve all staff has been made
throughout the previous chapters. The marketing function is a
necessary element of the management of educational institutions.
In keeping with the growing formalization of institutional planning, the organization of educational marketing should include the
following characteristics:

- the establishment of marketing objectives and an organizational
  framework for marketing;
- the systematic collection of marketing information through marketing audit and research;
- the development of a costed marketing plan, based upon the '5
  Ps', which forms part of the educational organization's corporate plan; and
- the implementation and evaluation of the strategies and tactics
  agreed in the plan.

This does no more than redirect a well-tried and long-
established approach to the management of education. Underlying
it is the fundamental belief that the education institution is there to
provide a service, and to respond to the needs of its pupils/students
and their parents and employers. The myth that the professionals

within the education service were uniquely qualified to identify and express those needs has been exploded. The 1988 Education Reform Act and its Scottish and Northern Irish equivalents formalized the myth's demolition. A more systematic approach to the marketing of educational provision is an inevitable response to demographic change and to government policies which increase competition in the public sector.

This does not require the wholesale imposition of alien business techniques and unsavoury salesmanship. Sound educational practice has long emphasized collegial responsiveness to student needs. A marketing perspective presents opportunities to listen all the more carefully to the views of students, and those who speak and act on their behalf, to respond effectively to criticisms, and to emphasize student choice in the face of the constraints imposed, for example, by the National Curriculum. A marketing perspective emphasizes the need for sound organization and for collegial approaches by teaching and non-teaching staff, whose involvement in and commitment to educational marketing will determine whether or not an educational institution succeeds, or even survives.

Finally, the required marketing skills include the redirection of some basic teaching skills, involving effective communication through a variety of media, tailored to customers whose needs have been carefully and skilfully analysed. Good marketing practice amounts to sound educational practice spiced by the adaptation of approaches effective in the marketing of other services. Schools and colleges now need to integrate these practices as central features of institutional management.

References

Ardrey, R. (1966). *The Territorial Imperative*. Collins, Glasgow.

Audit Commission (1984). *Obtaining Better Value in Education: Aspects of Non-teaching Costs in Secondary Schools*. HMSO, London.

Bell, J. (1987). *Doing Your Research Project*. Open University Press, Milton Keynes.

Bell, J., Bush, T., Fox, A., *et al.* (eds) (1984). *Conducting Small-scale Investigations in Educational Management*. Open University Press, Milton Keynes.

Borden, N. H. (1965). The concept of the marketing mix. In G. Schwartz (ed), *Science in Marketing*. John Wiley, Chichester.

BRAD (British Rate and Data) (monthly). McLean-Hunter.

Caldwell, B. and Spinks, J. (1988). *The Self-managing School*. The Falmer Press, Lewes.

Cameron, M., Rushton, R. and Carson, D. (1988). *Marketing*. Penguin, Harmondsworth.

Chartered Institute of Public Finance and Accountancy (1988). *Performance Indicators for Schools*. CIPFA, London.

Clift, P. S., Nuttall, D. L. and McCormick, R. (eds) (1987). *Studies in School Self-evaluation*. Falmer Press, Lewes.

Cowell, D. (1984). *The Marketing of Services*. Heinemann, London.

Davies, P. and Scribbins, K. (1985). *Marketing Further and Higher Education*. Longmans (for FEU and FESC), London.

Department of Education and Science (1987). *Higher Education: Meeting the Challenge*, Cm. 114. HMSO, London.

Department of Education and Science (1990a). *Standards in Education, 1988–89, The Annual Report of H.M. Senior Chief Inspector of Schools*. DES, London.

Department of Education and Science (1990b). *School Development Plans*. HMSO, London.

Department of Education and Science/Department of Employment (1984). *Training for Jobs*, Cmnd. 9135. HMSO, London.

Engel, J., Blackwell, R. and Miniard, P. (1986). *Consumer Behavior*, 5th edn. CBS College Publishing, Chicago.

Finegold, D. and Soskice, D. (1988). The failure of British training: Analysis and prescription. *Oxford Review of Economic Policy*, **4** (3), pp. 21–53.

Gorman, G. (1988). *Fund-raising for Schools*. Kogan Page, London.

Gray, L. (1983). *Managing Resources in Primary Schools*. Sheffield Papers in Education Management. Sheffield City Polytechnic, Sheffield.

Gray, L. (1984). Managing resources in schools and colleges. In S. Goulding, J. Bell, T. Bush *et al.* (eds), *Case Studies in Educational Management*, pp. 209–49, Harper and Row, London.

Gray, L. and Williams, A. (1990). *The Information Needs of Marketing Managers*. Marketing Network, London.

Handy, C. (1986). *Understanding Organizations*, 3rd edn. Penguin, Harmondsworth.

Heap, B. (1991). *The Complete Degree Courses 1992*. Trotman, Richmond-upon-Thames.

Hill, N. (1990). *Successful Marketing for Small Businesses*. Charles Letts & Co., London.

Holloway, J. C. and Plant, R. (1988). *Marketing for Tourism*. Pitman, London.

Keen, C. and Greenall, J. (1987). *Public Relations Management in Colleges, Polytechnics and Universities*. HEIST Publications, Banbury.

Kepner, C. and Tregoe, B. (1986). *The New Rational Manager*. McGraw-Hill, New York.

Knight, B. (1983). *Managing School Finance*. Heinemann, London.

Kotler, P. (1986). *The Principles of Marketing*, 3rd edn. Prentice-Hall, Englewood Cliffs, N.J.

Kotler, P. and Fox, A. (1985). *Strategic Marketing for Educational Institutions*. Prentice-Hall, Englewood Cliffs, N.J.

McDonald, M. (1989). *Marketing Plans*, 2nd edn. Heinemann, London.

McMahon, A., Bolam, R., Abbott, R., *et al.* (1984a). *Guidelines for Review and Internal Development in Schools: Primary School Handbook*. Longman, London.

McMahon, A., Bolam, R., Abbott, R., *et al.* (1984b). *Guidelines for Review and Internal Development in Schools: Secondary School Handbook*. Longman, London.

Megson, C. (1988). The merits of marketing. *Education*, **172** (16), p. 382.

National Association of Head Teachers (1990). *The Marketing of Schools*. NAHT, Haywards Heath.

Planning Exchange (for DES PICKUP) (annual). *Paying for Training, Planning Exchange*, Glasgow.

Powney, J. and Watts, M. (1987). *Interviewing in Educational Research*. Routledge, London.

Responsive College Programme (1988). Newsletter No. 3, Further Education Staff College, February.

Robinson, A. and Long, G. (1987). Marketing further education: Products or people? *NATFHE Journal*, March.

Robinson, A. and Long, G. (1988). Substance v. trappings in non-advanced FE. *Journal of Further and Higher Education*, **12** (1), Spring.

Scribbins, K. and Davies, P. (1989). Organising for marketing. *Management in Education*, **2** (1), Spring, pp. 11–21.

Sleight, S. (1990). *Sponsorship: What It Is and How to Use It*. McGraw-Hill, New York.

Task Group on Assessment and Testing (1988). *Report of the Task Group on Assessment and Testing*. DES, London.

Theodossin, E. (1989). *The Responsive College*. Further Education Staff College, Bristol.

Thomas, H. (1986). Choice in the education market. *Educational Management and Administration*, **14** (2), Summer, pp. 101–6.

Tilling, M. (1988). *Press and Public Relations in Education: A Practical Guide*. Sheffield Papers in Education Management 75, Sheffield City Polytechnic, Sheffield.

Torrington, D. and Weightman, J. (1989). *The Reality of School Management*. Blackwell, Oxford.

TRACE (1986). *Managing College Companies*. Wigan College of Technology, Wigan.

Walford, G. (1990). *Privatization and Privilege in Education*. Routledge, London.

Walker, J. and Hooper, R. (1988). *Going to Market*. Responsive College Programme, Preston.

Index